AF256372

# DAY TRADING

*The Beginners Guide to Invest and Make a Passive Income.*

*The Best Strategies to Maximize the Profit.*

William  Diamond

# Table of Contents:

## Introduction

This book is for individuals who are interested in starting out in day trading. You will get all the information you need, the basic and complex terms to know, and the tips and tricks in order to succeed. From the beginning, you'll have all the information that you will need to start off, from the meaning of day trading and the characteristics of a day trader. You will know if it is possible to rely on day trading as a source of income. You will know of the risks involved, what you need to by and when you will be able to sell. This might seem like a hectic process, you do not need to worry because the book will clearly explain the steps that you can take to ensure that you are comfortable when starting on day trading. You will know of the capital needed and how you will choose a broker. Money management is also important when it comes to day trading. You will know of the importance of money management, the helpful apps and the tips to use. Lastly, the common mistakes in day trading are illustrated to help in avoiding them. Do not worry about the terminologies and jargons used, they are all clearly illustrated. This topic is broad and there are several books available. Thank you for taking the time and picking this book as your final choice. All the efforts were put in to ensure you get a detailed and useful book. Enjoy your reading.

# Chapter 1: What is Day Trading?

## What is Day Trading?

Day trading is basically the purchasing and selling of securities within a single trading day in any marketplace at commonly stock markets and foreign exchange (FOREX) for the purpose of obtaining a compound of short term loans. Day traders involved in this are fully investing in this trading activity with multiple learning sources, learning time and good kind of capital often end up being so successful. Being successful in day trading literally means acquiring large chunks of profits amounts.

## Characteristics of a Day Trader

Being a day trader does come out naturally, a specific personality and traits are duly required. Below are some of the characteristics of a day trader.

□ Disciplined.

This is a major trait that day traders really need to input. Day traders should always be disciplined to remain input when no opportunities emerge and really act so fast when opportunities avail. Acting fast also includes strictly considering the step-by-step rules and obligations initially formed in their big plans.

□ Open-minded.

Day trading is a learning kind of income-generating engagement, implying that there are going to be happy times and the downfalls. Save yourself and learn from all that. Improve the happy times and completely discard the downfall wrong moves. Being exposed to the winnings and the failures makes you open-minded, master of all possible win moves.

☐   A fan of technology.

Day trading is carried out in various trading platforms and systems that a trader should be familiarized with. This should not scare you. Getting to know how they work does not, in any case, require you to be a computer whiz. Get to learn the basic moves and grow technologically with time.

☐    Mentally tough.

Losing market trades are constant; most successful traders will have losing trades every single day. They typically win slightly more times than they lose. It is so important too stay focused and rational during a losing period and do not let in the basic fact that money has been lost too. Focus on the future day trading activities by implementing some of the strategies outlined in a big plan.


☐    Independence.

Independence is striving to build your own toolbox that is and willy forever lead you. Reading trading books to trading books, watching each and every video, interacting with one mentor after the other can be a total miss. What if different books have one confusing point on a particular field? What is your YouTube subscriber who decides to quit vlogging? Always grasp the basics after in-depth research and day stay put. Dare to yourself that you got you and get the large chunks of benefits. However, when you feel you are so lost, do not hesitate to get assistance. Most importantly, master and analyze successful moves and let them be part of your big plan.

☐ Patience.

Good things do take quite some time. In every strategical move, you try to make, think about it carefully but this should not make you paranoid. Act accordingly with many disciplines to reduce the number of losses likely to be incurred during various day trading activities.

Also, a patient day trader is a learning day trader. Day trading is not going to be easy at first but with time, where you will be equipped with lots of skills and experience, things are expected to flow very smoothly. Hey, be patient.

☐    Future-oriented.

Getting stuck in the past makes you much of a prisoner. Forward-thinking lets you see the possible moves and gives you the decisive air when the next trading activity will occur considering the set protocols set in the day trader's plan. Being future-oriented incites forward thinking which is basically clearly involves mental thinking and knowing your next possible moves after a considerate examination. Being future-oriented hastens and simplifies the day trading operation moves and chances are that they are going to be successful.


☐    Financial freedom.

Day trading does not require you to be a tycoon necessarily but you are required to have a specific amount of money that has been precisely selected to begin day trading with. Remember the first times are always a win or loss situation as you continue to learn and grow. This particular set of money can be lost too. Be careful about how you handle your finances in day trading.

Not every story is a good story.


☐   Enthusiasm.

A great interest in something is a pending successful goal. A great enthusiastic inclination to stocks, securities, commodities, markets, the business gives you the thirst to learn and master what day trading is all about. These are signs of a future successful day trader.


☐   Experience and familiarity.

Experience comes with pretty much of downfall lessons and learning. Expose yourself to different learning sources and master every profitable move during day trading so as to squeeze out the best out of that. Getting the actual experience and familiarity of the trading platforms and various strategies needed to be successful at day trading is worthwhile.

## Difference between Long and Short Trade

In stock markets, the terms long and short basically imply whether a trade was initiated by first selling or first purchasing. A long trade is initiated when the day trader purchases at a particular price and with the intention of selling at a higher price in future in a bid to get profits whereas short trades are initiated with selling, before even purchasing with the intention of repurchasing at a lower price from the market and eventually acquire profits.

Short selling is simply:
Borrow the stock. Sell the stock.
Buyback the stock? Profit or loss?

Risks are also involved during short selling; stock prices may end up being so high and normally, there is no limit to how a particular price can actually go.

During long trading, your profit potential is unlimited since the price of the asset can rise indefinitely.

## Can One Do Day Trading for a Living?

The first point to take down is yes, day trading is a lucrative engagement. However, that does not mean that it is way simple than any other actual job. And yes, you get to be your own boss. You get to do it your way, on your time, with your strategies for a living. It is amazing. We do not get so lucky in this life though, drawbacks have to appear too. Below, let us venture on the different pros and cons that come with day trading.

Benefits:

- Own boss

Getting to work the way you desire has always been the best thing ever. Your plan, your moves, your strategies. This is so good. Imagine going for a wanting vacation without first passing through the Human Resource department with some great explanation so that your reason can be valid enough. Moreover, getting to work for you already gives you the full energy to make things really alive. You have enough spirit to learn and bring out the best in you. Do yourself a huge favor and be your own boss.

- Comfort.

A peaceful working environment enhances the quality of the end product, or rather, the aftermath turns out to be so successful. A peaceful environment creates a much-concentrated workspace, day traders get to strictly master the actual day trading activities and learn more every day. This will at the end accomplish their big plans as indicated by the large chunks of profits that would be made.

- Risk management.

Exposure to day-to-day cases of day trading will definitely make you a better risk-taker. Day trading is made up of so many risks that act as a day-to-day lessons. The trader gets to master the good moves and discard the previously made mistakes so as to become a successful day trader.

- Technologically advantaged.

Day trading exposes you to the internet as you try to get access to various sources. The internet is technology, so full of technology. You are exposed to new sites and different technological techniques. This builds you because technology is the present and the future.

Drawbacks:

- A solitary lifestyle.

Day trading is a peace of mind activity implying that physical noise should not be part of it. This creates a lonely kind of environment since the trader is mostly by his or herself trying to master the possible good moves. You are really going to enjoy day trading if the best company is normally just your company.

- Inconsistent salary figure.

Your smart trading work will be reflected by the salary figure you obtain every single trading day. When you decide to take a day off, no gains are promised. At one particular point, you may gain like $3000 and the next day you experience $2000 loss, no consistent salary figures are promised, your smart moves are the ones that will get you a Lamborghini.

## How to Decide on What and When to Buy

When and what exactly to buy in day trading is so fundamental. Let us outline some of the factors that need to be considered.

☐ Understand the level of risk is involved and what kind of risk level is suitable for you.

There is a bunch of stocks to trade with different rates of volatility, price and volume characteristics. There are different kinds of risks experienced in each and every level of day trading. As a beginner, pick the risk level that matches your risk management rate. Day to day trading activities exposes you to several kinds of risks that occur frequently so every trading day becomes a learning day. With time, a beginner is exposed to all kinds of possible risks that are likely to be educative and he or she gets to be a pro in handling risks.

- Analyze and come up with the right kinds of prices to buy.

Your personality totally describes you and therefore, judging from it, you should favor your self with the kind of day market you want to get involved in. For instance, if you have a fast mind yet you can really focus despite the string of actions needed at a particular circumstance, you should go for short term trading.

- Focus and analyze a particular stock.

Keep it simple. Deal with a particular stock at a time. Understand how it is handled, explore all its sides and examine how it is operated at multiple time frames Every stock has its own characteristics and personality meaning that

you need to understand its behavior in order to anticipate the right moves.

- Explore several trading charts to understand the stock movement and the overall market performances.

Charts act as a pictorial representation of the actual activities that are taking place in the day trading market. They help to monitor and express every moment taking place during trading. A beginner is obliged to master and learn every move that is depicted from the charts for future successful moves in day trading.

☐   Be disciplined and strictly stick with your

plan. Strictly following up the initial strategical set plan is a successful move-in day trading. Being disciplined enough to follow what was examined and noted down as a step guarantees the day trader the zero chances of incurring large chunks of losses.

☐   Time frame.

Traders spend almost 30 seconds in choosing a time frame, not because of their trading technique or trading market, but basically by just their own personality. For instance, traders with an intention of making so many trades during the day end up choosing shorter time frames while traders with an intention of making like two to three trades in a particular trading day pick longer time frames. Time frames are not really constant in the trading day since the activeness of the trader in that particular day says it all.

## Deciding When to Sell

☐     Mental fatigue.

Brain fatigue incites poor trading performances that correspond to long strings of stop losses. Trading for just two or three hours keeps you set in your game and the chances of excelling in your trading activities are pretty much high.

☐     Trading at the opening.

Novice is advised not to engage in the first 15 minutes of a new trading day. It is believed by most seasoned traders that at this period, a lot of dumb money is really initiated. Dumb money is simply the actual amount of capital that most traders use as they sell and buy market prices based on the immediate previous trading episodes during the start of their trading day.

Professional day traders are advantaged in this particular morning.

☐ Ending trading by 11.30

10.30 am ET is considered to be the best day trading period. It offers the biggest moves in the shortest amount of time. Well, you can decide to extend an hour since that is when volatility and volume tend to tamper off

☐ The last hour.

Most traders are likely to trade the last hour, which is from 3 pm to 4 pm ET. This period is recommended because most traders have had a long break session since then and are likely to have resurfaced and really focused. The last hour is much like the first hour, where a lot of dumb money can be depicted as many traders try to unfold how the day like likely to end based on the happenings during the day. The last hour of the day can really be active with such big moves on high volumes.

☐   Best day and month.

A lot recommend that Friday might the best day to trade before that Monday dip happens mostly if it the first Friday of the month or when it precedes a three-day weekend.

**Risks Involved in Day Trading**

☐   Financial breakdown.

It is so advisable that you interact with the kind of capital that you are ready to lose. Due to the meager time frame during day trading, prices fluctuate from time to time. The amount traded with is not so predictable and it can be easily subjected to a major loss. Be careful with how you handle your finances, the financial breakdown can too be a possible option.

Also, day traders must also payday trade firms commissions and tutorial costs to be subjected to the trainers. Day trading is cost-effective.

☐　Margin borrowing.

Margin borrowing is basically the loan amount you acquire for the essence of purchasing securities. The amount is likely to grow from the impacted interest and potentially put the trader in a position of over-borrowing. It is highly recommended that the trader should clearly comprehend how margin borrowing goes about before trading on borrowed capital.

☐　Market movements.

The market moves in less than a hundred points in either direction in a single trading day. Traders normally spotting each and every market move are likely to acquire higher rates of profits in that they are able to observe and act on several moves happening and they may be after all be successful. Being late on a trade can definitely convert a potential profit to a loss. Try to stay updated on what is actually happening in the trade market.

☐ Psychological addiction.

Day trading is considered to weigh the same in addition to gambling. Day trading is highly addictive since the traders are said to eventually turn out competitive and of above-average intelligence.

☐ Slippage risk.

This kind of risk involves hidden costs that are normally associated with every transaction. It normally takes place anytime in the market but mostly when you are using orders during high volatile times. It also occurs when you place huge orders on assets with less interest in purchasing.

Slippage risks mostly affect forex and stock traders in the market. Try your best to avoid slippage risks by using limit orders in trading rather than market orders.

☐ Risks of over-trading.

Overtrading occurs in several circumstances. You may incur over trading in the aspect of trying to recover for the made losses. Another way, you may try to average your positions when stop losses are approaching and end up causing over-trading. Try to avoid such risks in all aspects.

☐ Stock selection.

Stock selection is so fundamental in day trading. If you get your stock selection wrong, this is going to be so wrong for you. Select stocks that are quite liquid and exhibit clear trading patterns that are going to work for you. Wrong stock selection incurs large chunks of losses which will most probably diminish you.

☐   Technical analysis.

Technical analysis is not a perfect science. Assumptions that past patterns are likely to repeat are never good assumptions, and which in many cases incur to major risk of stop losses triggering on either side of the trade.


☐   Market volatility.

Market volatility is the norm in market day trading. Even with your best-set strategies and well-picked kind of stock, day trading episodes are not really predictable. External macro factors at day trading make the market volatile triggering a string of stop losses and after all, you end up putting your day trading capital at a bigger risk.


☐   Emotional trading.

Again, failing to plan is planning to fail. Some of the day traders target the hot stocks probably recommended by several spam email reports in the belief of acquiring major profits. Okay, a turn of events is likely to unfold. Day trading is a kind of systematic income-generating activity. A strategical plan with major points to note when handling day trading should be formulated. It ought to guide you on several major day trading moves, mistakes, and their solutions, and also updated keywords he or she learns as day trading keeps advancing.

☐ Trading with small amounts.

There is a limit that has been set to day trading. Slightly bigger limits are recommended to avoid many risks from being incurred.

# Chapter 2: Basic Concepts of Day Trading

Traditionally, most of the people who used to trade in the stock market were those who work in brokerages, trading houses, and financial institution.

Thanks to the influx of technology and the internet, there has been a rise in online trading places. Brokers have taken advantage of that and individuals are able to play the games online. This is also the reason why many people are aware of day trading. This has turned out to be a rising and lucrative business. The secret is to make sure that you completely understand what it entails, practice and learn more. For the newbies, it can be a little bit challenging. You do not need to worry since with the right strategy, approach and plan you are bound to succeed. What you should know is that even the most experienced day traders have their failures and a bad day. First, you need to know how day trading works.

## How Does Day Trading Work?

What you should know is that day trading is not an investment. It involves purchasing an asset stake hopefully to make a profit over a set period. The length of time to anticipate the profit is subjective. This is because most investors are always open to the idea of holding their assets for many years, which can end up to decades. The secret is to be aware of the industry you are investing in. Always look for firms that are known to make great profit margins. They are the best since your profitability and great returns are guaranteed. Look for firms that are debt-free, have a strong product line, and do not have any pending lawsuits.

Day traders will buy and sell financial securities within a day. Traders will look for different sources of funds to buy the securities. Most of them will borrow funds and buy when the security prices are lower anticipating them to rise later in the day. The basic principle is to always buy when the cost is low and sell when it is high. That is where you will get the best profit margins.

This s always managed at a compressed time limit.

An example is when a trader buys around 500 shares at 9:00 am. After 30 minutes, the price goes up, and he decides to sell. He will end up making a profit for that day less the commission chargeable and any applicable taxes. You need to know that when you sell a stock or investment that you have owned for less than a year. It is normally taxed against your personal gains. They are taxed at 35% as opposed to the long-term ones that are taxed at around 20%. It is evident that when day trading, you should put into consideration the taxation concept.

The beauty of day trading is that you have the ability to have at least 25 trades per day. The profit margin will increase based on the number of trades.

Day traders always limit their risks, by not owning their stock overnight to avoid drastic price changes. The main reason could be market volatility hence the need for immediate response. Day traders will act quickly and make fast decisions, unlike other traders who will take time to make any decision.

**What does a Day Trader do?**

Day trader's typical day involves participating in financial markets purchasing and disposing of stocks, forex, and other securities. Their work also involves closing positions in order to make small and regular profits. There are different types of traders. The small-scale ones, the independent ones with their home space, and the ones based in institutions. Apart from trading, they also manage and maintain different markets and do research. They also do an analysis of financial notes based on securities and exchange information with the other traders.

This type of trading is considered to be on the fast

lane and requires someone who can handle a lot of challenges and stress. You will need a deep and clear understanding of how the market works. You will also need to possess the required trading skills to be successful. One of the skills includes the ability to analyze different price charts.

A day trader always starts its day before the financial markets open. They will check all the financial information to help in economic development, analytical reports, market data, and any political news. They also check and do an analysis of the technical indicators and any results from the trading.

The information they rely upon is from their subscription and analyst. This information is crucial and helps in decision-making.

The other duty for a day trader is to check any confirmations from trading. The confirmation is from the trading from the previous day. Then they check any activity notes and the overnight position that they hold. In case there are any errors, they need to be fixed immediately. Since all the charges are billed to the trader.

Then they will ensure that the trades have been successfully settled. The next thing will be to check the cash that the got and the profit in their

trading account. What they confirm is if there is a purchase that was not sent to their accounts. Or a third party to a sale who has not paid for the security. They need to immediately address that since it is bound to affect their trading ability.

The most important part of a trader's life is when the market opens. The trader will put all the orders in the open that is entirely dependent on their style and plans. Then they will enter follow-ups on the trades that they intend to sell or buy. They spend the most part of the day doing analysis. Analyzing financial reports and charts with price movements. An hour before the market closes; the trader will then close all the positions before leaving for the day.
This is to ensure that there are no overnight risks.

Making a profit is any trader's goal. When they are private traders, they will bank all the profit. For the employed ones, they earn a percentage of the gains since they trade under customers' accounts. When there is a loss, nothing is paid. In fact, they need to refund the cash advances to the trading account.

Other duties of a day trader include doing market analysis and observation. Trading strategies formulation and completing a trade with brokers. They ensure that they sell all assets by the close of the day and have the investment as cash and profits. They also cut losses when there is a failure in investment. They are required to complete tax returns and do transaction recording.

## Techniques Used in Day Trading

You need to have the best techniques when it comes to trading. Day trading can be considered simple or complicated based on the techniques and approaches that you use. Ensure that you are familiar with the concept and all that it entails. The best techniques are the ones that will help in maximizing profit and minimize price movements. In order to have effective approaches, you will need to depend on in-depth analysis, use price charts, and price indicators. The patterns will help in predicting price changes in the future.

This chapter will illustrate the best strategies and techniques to adopt that will help all traders on a different level; from beginners to experts. You will be able to know how to position yourself and know about the resources that are useful. The important thing to note is ensuring that you pick a technique that will perfectly fit with your preference, requirements, and style.

When you are starting out in the world of trading, do not be n a hurry to master all the technical terms and processes. Starts with the basics first; do not think that having a complicated technique is what will make you successful. You should know that the simpler your plan is the more effective it will be.

☐ You need to understand all the components of money management. You need to know the amount of money you are ready to risk as your capital. Note that it is not advisable to put down anything above 2% of your capital for each trade. Ensure that you are aware that you are also bound to make losses.

☐ Ensure you know how to manage your time. Day trading will need you to input a lot of your time. And you should also know how to strike a balance between your professional and personal life. Do not expect to allocate like an hour or two, and expect to have great returns. Be attentive in monitoring the financial markets and looking for new trading chances.

☐ Start small, do not be in a hurry to invest a lot of capital. Learn a lot, master the skill then invest more. You can start with at least 3 stocks daily. It is considered wise to start with fewer stocks and make great returns that investing in more and not gaining anything.

☐ The only way to understand the market and master it is by learning a lot. You need to keep yourself informed on what is happening. Be updated on what is happening, any news or occasions. Ensure you know about asset implications especially when there is a shift in economic policies.

☐ Be consistent with your trading. Deliver work with the same morale and spirit. Depend on logical facts and a strategic plan. Always ensure that your timing is always right. This is because when the market opens, it becomes volatile. Experts will be able to read the patterns, you should be able to bide the time. You can hold on in the first minutes of trading.

There are several components that each trader is s meant to know. Be it a beginner or experienced, you should master the components.

**Volatility**: This component will illustrate the potential gain in each trade. Great volatility means greater gains or losses.

**Liquidity**: This component makes a trader enter and exit the trading period and still manage a stable and attractive price.

**Volume**: Volume is a component that will indicate the number of times a stock has been traded over a certain time. It is commonly known as the average daily trading volume. When the volume is high, it indicates higher gains or interest in the trade. When the volume increases, it means that there is a change in price.

## What is the Market to Day Trade?

There are three different markets for day trading. They are forex, futures, and stock market. Most people are aware of the stock market and not future and forex.

**Stock Market**: When people think of day trading, stock market comes into their mind first. It is considered the best when it comes to buying and selling company shares. And you'll need to exit all positions by the close of the trading period. There is a requirement to hold at least $25k in your account, anything less will not be accepted in day trading. The required capital to start is $30k.

**Future Market**: This is another market for day trading. This is where there is an agreement between a seller and a buyer. They agree to sell or buy at an agreed amount at a certain time. Traders make their gains from price fluctuations. This is from the difference computed between what is bought or sold and when the position closes. For this market, you do not need too much capital, a minimum of $3500 and a maximum of $5k is enough to start. The opening hours vary, you need to be careful and ensure that before the trade closes, you are out. You need to consider access to the future market and know of the requirements. Usually, there is a limit on the minimum balance; it is set at $2k.

**Forex Market**: This is considered a common and accessible market; it trades for 24 hours in a day. They are allowed to start with a minimum capital of around $100, what is recommended is at least $500 to start with. They only deal with one currency and that could be a limitation when it comes to the investment currency. There are also specifications and requirements for this trading platform. As a trader, you need to be careful of the platform that you choose, ensure it is something that fits your preferences and needs. There are demo accounts that can be used to practice and apply the techniques you have learned.

Several factors will affect your choice for a trading market. They include your financial position, the trading technique that, interests and personality. An example is when you want to start trading and your capital is below $25k. You will not be able to trade unless you continue saving up. When your capital is adequate, you can choose any of the trading markets listed above.

You need to know that there are other techniques that will work in one market and not the other.

And others will work in a certain time and others not. Always When you have a technique to adopt, choose one market and stick to that. When you are new to day trading, do not flip between markets but maintain a market. You are allowed to shift between trades based on the time you are trading.

All three markets are considered great. You will choose a market based on your preference and interest. However, it is recommended to stick to one market, as you know more about the others.

# What is the Expected Monthly Income from Day Trading?

Most people start day trading for different reasons. To some it is just a lifestyle, others business and others love the challenge. The amount of money that day traders make vary, some will lose capital will others will use it to gain more income. How the trader makes their income is influenced by the approach they use and how they manage their risk. The secret to more income is to have a better approach, ensure you are able to manage your risk and work hard.

Most traders will ensure that their risk is small, equivalent to at least 1 % of the capital they use to trade in with. If you are trading with stock worth $3000, ensure that your risk is not more than $30.

The strategy that is used in trading is normally in two categories: the win rate and the profit that is relative to losses. The win rate is described as the number of times a trader wins. And then you need to divide that by a number of trades. For instance, when a strategy wins at 60 trades from 100 trades. That will be at 60%. Having a high win rate is every trader's wish. But that will not make you profitable if your wins are high, but fewer winners that are not considered profitable. The win rate is expected to be at least 50%. And the reward to risk ratio is a factor that needs to be considered. In any given time, traders will expect to have bigger winners than losers.

Even though day trading is the most common and known, it also requires more capital investment. Let's assume a day trader starts their trading at $40k, and you use a 4:1 ratio. It will give a buying power of $160k (4 x $40k), ensure you have a reward to risk ratio is 1.5:1. This will be in terms of $0.15 as winning trades and $0.10 as losing trades. This means that the maximum loss you can encounter is $400, which is 1% of $30k. To achieve that, you will need to trade with stocks that have high volatility and volume.

When you choose a good strategy in your trading, you are guaranteed 50% of the profit. So if you have 5 trades daily, and you trade 20 days per month; that is an equivalent of 100 trades monthly. So that will be computed as 50 x $0.15 x 4000 = $30,000. And if the other half was a loss, that will be 50 x $0.10 x 4000 = $20,000. So your gain will be $10,000 and you'll need to deduct commission chargeable and some other fees.

Another example is when the trade cost is $10, the commission will be 100 trades by $10= $1000. Your take-home will be $10,000 - $1000 = $9,000 per month.

# Day Trading Hardware Requirements

For you to be a successful day trader there are several tools of the trade that are required. You might already possess some of them. Modern trading is mostly done online, and you will be able to view and access financial markets on the internet and have access to the trades. Therefore, the first equipment you will need is s a laptop or a computer. Then organize how you will be accessing your internet. There will come a time when you will need to call your broker for clarification or update. At that point, you will need a phone to be able to do that.

You will also need access to brokerage, market data in real-time, and chart for trading. All this will enable you to run your trades effectively and smoothly. Day trading needs advance and updated technology. So when getting a laptop or computer ensure you get one with enough memory and a faster processor to avoid any lagging or crashing. Ensure that the machine s faster when it comes to loading information. If you get that your workload is constantly increasing, you can invest in two desktops.

When you have a problem with your internet, the only way you can communicate with your brokers will be via a phone call. Ensure you invest in a phone or landline for trading purposes. As a backup tip, ensure you program your broker's number on your phone. So that when you do not have access to the internet or your computer breaks down, you can access their number.

To succeed in day trading, you will need a broker; a company that helps in the facilitation of the trades. Day traders do a lot of trades on a daily basis, this is why they need a broker who will charge low commissions and the best trading software. There are brokers that are known from banks, but the problem is they charge high commission and do not have solutions tailor-made for day traders. Day traders are advised to always seek services of brokers who are small scale and regulated. Make sure if you choose software that is compatible with the brokers.

You will need to have access to accurate financial information and data. Most of them are derived from price movements and changes from the assets and markets they are trading in. You'll need to request the information that you need from the broker. You will get some brokers giving information free but in return, the commission charges are high. The basic requirements are a quick and reliable laptop or desktop, a working telephone, and software for trading. You should consider getting a smartphone that can use backup internet. Plan for reliable and fast internet connectivity and find a broker who is regulated. One who charges commissions that are low and will provide trading software. The last thing will be to subscribe to market information of your choice based on the trading market.

## Day Trading Software Requirements

The trading charts require a processor and a memory component; they should be of high speed and updated. Do not go for software that will make your screen to freeze once you become busy analyzing your trades. Look for internet connectivity that is fast enough to help in loading web pages. If that is not possible, consider your internet slow to do any day trading. When there are price movements and changes, you will be getting thousands of information to your computer. The streaming is done per second. Therefore, that means it is a lot of data per hour for a day.

When it is too slow to do all that, you will have a lag experience. Lag simply means, receiving old data instead of new. You will have data backlog and not able to see any current prices. Take a test from all the internet providers before making a choice.

Always consider having internet access with a backup plan. This will help when there is an internet outage, you will still be able to access the internet. This can be done easily using a smartphone, via hot spot or mobile data. The backup plan should be outsourced from a company different from the internet provider. So that when the internet connectivity goes done, it will not affect the backup plan.

# Chapter 3: How to Start Day Trading

Day trading is becoming a lucrative engagement in the commerce industry with recent technological advancement. Hey there, welcome to the stock market world. This end is strategically oriented and plenty of fat risks coming your way. Let's dive into some of the factors that are likely to be considered.

## The Capital Needed to Start Day Trading

Capital is so necessary to set the actual day trading ball on fire. Acquiring loans from different sites has been revealed to be so common among traders. With this glue on the mind, traders tend to be so careful with the amount of capital that they actually intend to commence with. To begin, traders are ought to obtain ready capital so as to monitor any kind of slight changes that are

presumed to occur during the course of the day.
Day trading requires a minimum account balance
of $1000, but $8000- $10,000 is recommended
by many providers and plenty of traders are not
willing to risk 1% from the value. Also, the $1000
minimum amount that can be implemented can
lead to your trading activities in being so not
worthwhile. Step by step kind of beginning

is so vital because you get to acquire progress
constantly and get to grow at a good speed with
messing things out.


**Choosing a Broker**


Once you have set your mind on exactly what
intend to trade, a broker should be following up in
mind. Brokers are the navigators of several trading
investment platforms. Bearing this I mind, we
ought to be super perfect in choosing a broker
because they reflect reliability, reputations, and

expertise in your trading account.

Let us look at some of the ways that are set to be considered:

☐   Really decide on what you will be trading.

Experts get their names by being good (perfect) in a particular field of trading. A stocks broker may be so bad in FOREX trading and vice versa. All the best in picking the best and the right one.

☐   Sourcing for recommendations.

Sticking in mind that the actual amount of money to be used during trading is really your own money, a wake-up call is assured and a good broker who can't be dodging with your precious money is super needed.

Try to even inquire from your colleagues you may have been in the previous spot or who they may have heard of good brokers. Try to also have some in- depth research from varieties of social media content, online reviews on the investment platforms, discussion boards and also take plenty of time to examine their websites.

Once you get several references, don't hesitate to check on their trading platforms. How were their actions? Any available complaints? How many traders have they ever been engaged with? How long have they been doing this? Have they been following the rules and regulations needed as a broker?

☐    Commissions rate.

Despite the fact that the "perfect" broker is super needed as you begin day trading, consider in mind that this is also a new project as a whole. Meaning that profits too, need to be made so as this whole project can exist for a long while. Consider the rates of commissions that are likely to be spent so as to avoid any losses from being made. Pick an economical one so as to really save yourself.

☐    Executive Speed.

Any delay of seconds can result in a massacre to a trader's profits. To prevent this, the broker should really make sure that the trading activities are at a top- notch. The broker should be able to quickly spot any rapid changes that are likely to be incurred in the trading platforms.

☐    Charting strategies.

Getting great chatting tools and software is also fundamental. Make sure you are getting good trading strategies, reliable variable markets, and better software features to enhance good day trading

☐    Paper trading.

It's advisable to begin day trading with paper trading, where you won't have to use your own money, though many brokers highly discourage this. Know where your heart takes you.

☐    Technology.

So, is the broker up for the new technological advancements? What kinds of accounts do they deal with? Does he/she have a real-time-data feed so that you can easily track and monitor trading activities? Which safeguard trading and Cybersecurity measures do they follow during trading? What kind of volumes of trading can they handle?

Greatly consider the kind who's so updated with the current technological happenings and pretty much informed.

☐    Customer service provision.

Are they willing to offer customer service services? What happens when your system during mid-trade and it costs you so much? Are they going to support you so as to get much out of trading? Which process are they going to utilize during complaint resolution? And many more. Consider these before signing the contract because it's a big deal.

☐    Safe, secure and regulated.

It's such a marvelous idea to inquire about the security of the broker in question. Inquire on how long they have been in business, their past work reports, what measures they have been using and their recent big measures on day trading.

Make sure they regulated by an agency and that they strictly value and consider the rules and regulations needed to be followed by any broker engaged in day trading.


☐    Adequate support.

Engage with brokers that are willing to provide huge support once there is a miss during your daily training activities. A few cents incremented on the broker's commission accounts is much worthwhile compared to hundreds of dollars losses that are likely to be incurred on the bad days.

## How to Become a Day Trader

The following basic tools are recommended:

### Computer/Monitor.

Well, cheap is expensive. A slow kind of computer can cause you a great fortune. Slow working definitely implies that the day trading tracks to be unreliable and totally not trending. This is really going to cost you in that the rates of profits at the end of any activity will be way low. They can cause you to miss trades, therefore, making your idea so unreliable. Remember you have a good reputation to uphold.

With all these in mind, please bear a quite fast laptop or monitor.

### Set a target, really motivating.

Setting a realistic trading target is going to manage

and monitor your real cash big time. A certain target is put for the purpose of big motivation. Work on that. Be for it big time. Remember achieving your target is normally tough because we all have really "dream" targets. Consistent losses will be incurred too, so prepare to lose some cash. Failure is never good though and will never be, So keep up champ!

**Create a demo account.**

Rehearsing has been always been a good move as your head to be successful navigation. Set up a demo account that will help you master all the ropes and moves that are likely to be incurred. Reading the fluctuations, the market trends are one way of future taking master moves that are great chances for high profitability rates. Keep testing and practicing until you are sure that you indeed set to go. Examine the market.

Master most of the trading moves. This makes you informed and definitely enhances specialization in a particular field.

## Fast internet connection.

A constant, fast and reliable type of internet connection is highly recommended. The unreliable internet connection can cause a miss in the market trends that can hinder the trading traces in a way leading to major losses being incurred at the end. Most of the users use a cable and ADSL type of connection. Remember that day trading does not recommend any unreliable source of connection.

## Type of market.

As discussed earlier, each kind of day trading demands a different kind of day trading. Choosing the kind of market to start with is super important, choose the most preferred.

**Discover the tax implications likely to be incurred.**

Inquire on how taxes revolve around profits. Engage with your financial adviser to let him or her explain how taxes are handled. Are they going to cause a devaluation on the made profits? Are they good news? How does that happen?

Be informed so as to at the end the trader can guess on the likelihood net profits to be expected.

**Choose the right stocks to trade.**

Well, to be better in choosing the right kind of stock, doing some in-depth research on the current existing stock is way the first step. Get to know the kind of stocks that are likely to perform well. Most preferably, those that are likely to perform well on a day-to-day basis. Remember to at least try one or two different kinds of stock until you are so sure that you have picked out the right one.

**Plan a good financial figure.**

You will need to prepare yourself early enough on the amount of money that can be risked on the day trading business. It is mostly advised not to risk more than 1-2% of your account money so as to avoid future losses.

Another piece of advice to the beginners, stay away from trading on the margin until you are set with enough moves and good trading wisdom. This will save you some extra cash in time.

**Know the lingo.**

Becoming an expert clearly requires much effort. There are certain keywords that you are required to be familiar with. Check them out:

- Ask the amount of money a trader is offering for sale.

- Know the bid: This is the money amount a trader is ready to purchase. Stock breakouts:

Declaring a stock that has experienced a breakout, basically talks of its reduction in the level of resistance.

- Candlestick: This is a type of chart specifically for prices that shows the maximum, minimum, opening and closing prices for a specified period of time.

- Covering: This refers to the buying back of the trade shares that had been sold earlier to do away with the obligation.

- Float: This is the amount of market share that is ready for day trading. Stock Gap Up or Down: This normally occurs when the price of a market trade becomes more or less than its previous closing price.

- The idea of Going Long: This normally refers to buying a market trade with the objective of offering it for sale at a higher price.

- High of Day and Low of Day: This is the highest or the lowest price a market trade has traded throughout the day.

- Hard to borrow list: This is ideally a list used by brokers that tells the stocks that are hard to borrow for short term sales.

- Market liquidity: This is a term that describes the state of the market showing how fast an inventory can be sold or purchased without affecting its price.

- Low Float Stock: This is basically a type of stock with a low amount of shares available for trading.

- Market Maker: This term generally refers to any market participant, be it a firm or an individual who can purchase, sell and clear market trades. A market maker normally operates under given by-laws of a country.

- Market Capitalization: This refers to the overall value of shares and stock of a business center. Most specifically ordinary shares (unit of capital).

- Outstanding Shares: This is a type of shares that have been given out by a company and have been subscribed by shareholders. They are normally shown as share capital in the company's balance sheet.

- The P&L (Profits and Losses): This is a financial statement, also referred to as an income statement. It indicates the revenue, costs, and expenses incurred by a business for a specified period of time normally a quarter a year.

- Red Green trading: The red and green colors on trading charts also have meaning. The green bar indicates the stock which is higher compared to the previous day. The red bar scenario shows the stock which closed lower that day as compared with the previous day.

- Resistance: This is the price point of stock which is normally at a higher level. The price level overpowers buyers, making it hard for the inventory to have a price increase.

- Scalping: Considering every small price ranges that are likely to happen during day trading.

- Short Selling: This activity involves selling off some shares at a price that is likely to make a good profit when buying them later.

- Spread: This is the price bridge between the bid and asks during day trading.

- Support trading. This is a section in a trading chart that indicates where price had dropped and tried it best to break below.

- Technical Analysis: Historical analysis of the price of the stock is involved with the use of mechanisms like charts so as to predict possible outcomes in the future.

- Top trends: This is an actual graphical representation of the stock's movement within trading while monitoring the top trends and downtrends. Trends are so important in day trading because they give the brokers and traders a sense of a particular direction and makes them informed of all moves and plan for better strategies.

**Venture into several day trading courses to get educated.**

Before getting involved in a particular course of study, kindly consider the following tips:

☐ The course should be taught by a professional.

Ignoring his/her profession, just pick out a teacher who happens to be an expert in a specific trading field. Why? So as to acquire detailed, accurate, reliable and up-to-date pieces of information. This will so motivate you in your trading journey.

☐ Availability of educational support tools.

The presence of proper educational tools will give the learner an audience to readily grasp every fundamental piece of information. The professional should also be ready to face time or live chat with any student who really needs great help.

☐ Based on your particular field.

Well, we agreed on picking out a particular trading sector field and really working on it. Well, your educational source should go hand in hand in whatever field that you have selected. Make sure that the learning source is detailed so as to acquire a bigger piece of information.

☐ High rated learning the source.

A perfectly detailed piece of learning information entails that a lot has been covered. Go for that. We have to make our day trading journeys so well, then meaning that our start-off spots should be good.

Putting all these in mind, take a look at some awesome sources for beginners:

Books and journals.
Online courses for day trading. Applications for games.

- Beginner level books for day trading.

**Perform a personal audit.**

Day trading is much of analytical work. A clear understanding of what is actually going to take place is so needed. Day trading is not a get-rich-overnight thing. It's a step by step learning project that involves simple to complex tactics that get to be implemented by the trader during his/her day trading journey.

**Set the right strategies.**

First things first, getting to know what you are actually working on is the most important activity. What do I want? How are you going to achieve all these? Is it worth it? How long is this going to take? What are the possible outcomes?

A little reminder, a proper strategical outline calls for hard work and patience so as to achieve an amazing goal. You got this!

## Chapter 4: Advice to Beginners on Day Trading

Day trading is not simple at first. Skills have to be built and some policies are set. All in all, it is a learning process that calls for patience and perseverance. Let us look at various fields at how you can get motivated this good day.

## Day Trading Strategies for Beginners

- ☐ **Financial analysis**: Well, money is a very important asset. With that in mind, you need to be super careful in how you plan on using it. Failing to plan is planning to fail. Beginners are advised to use just a little amount of capital for a start-up until the time they are fully experienced in the day trading track. Most of the traders do not have more than 2% of the capital in the trade. Furthermore, as a beginner always consider slow but sure steps. Get to grow little by little. This is a journey with lots and lots of protocols to learn and master with a successful and rich endpoint.

☐ **Seek every kind of learning material**: Learning makes you educated on what you are actually doing. It makes you informed, you get to learn every living trick in that particular field(day trading). Take each day as a learning day in that you get to learn something new in a particular section. You get to grow. Being involved in day trading is a course journey itself. Below are some sources of learning materials for day trading:

☐ **Videos:** Videos provide practical learning sources and that is why they end being so famous. Explore several video learning content from sites like YouTube.

☐ **Articles, blogs, etc**: Day traders from different places of the world like to engage their experiences from the moment they started trading. As a beginner, seek the beginner level kind of sources. Read their experiences widely, take down important facts, ask questions, recommendations. With that, even the confidence and the thrust force to begin day trading will highly be enlightened.

☐ **Trends**: Get to follow each and every trend and get the idea of what is actually happening. They are highly educative when it comes to future prediction analysis.

☐ **Consistency or stability:** Another idea to add, day trading is quite logical. Day trading can not be analyzed by fear or even greed.

Mathematical approaches have to be considered. Set strategies have to be put in place too! Examine every logical operation bound to happen during day trading so as to possess certain clear stability. Once stability has been established, expect some big-time profit rates and an excellent reputation.

☐ **Timing**: The trading market becomes volatile every single trading day. Experienced traders have mastered the moves and so they are quite sure about what steps to take next once they get to read the structures. For beginners? Quite not sure of what move to take. A slow but sure protocol is fundamental too. As a beginner, do not be quite in a rush to predict. Take one or more time to examine every single trend and get your desired prediction. Do not be too slow though, you may end missing so much.

☐ **Scalping:** Scalping kind of strategy takes advantage of the small kind of prices that happen drastically during the day trading sessions. This kind of mechanism involves getting engaged so quickly and so fast and then leaving right away.

## Day Trading Charts and Patterns

Charts and patterns are very important visual measures in day trading. They entail progress and updates of each and everyday trade and traders use it to determine whether it is going to be a win or a loss during their activities.

They are also used as a tool to predict future trading activities. Below are some of the charts and patterns that are used in day trading:

- Line chart.

The use of Line charts is one of the most famous types of charts in use. They only show the closing price for that period.

A continuous line will be drawn from a single closing price to the next immediate closing price.

A line chart usually assists in bringing forth important information and making it easier to notice previous price points. However, it is inadvisable to base your principal determiners' online chart's data as it lacks crucial information.

- Use of Bar charts.

These charts are made up of two kinds of lines; vertical and horizontal lines. Vertical lines will reflect the price range under a given period of time whereas the horizontal lines cover prices on opening and closing. In certain cases where the opening price ends up being lower than the closing price, the produced line will usually be black and/ or red, for vice versa. Bar charts are believed to be an expression towards line charts and they offer reliable and accurate information during reading and interpretation as compared to line charts.

Bar charts are much detailed, with plenty of information and therefore so easy to read and interpret and preferred by most traders.

Bar charts are composed of open feet as they face to the left, vertical line and a closing foot produced that directs to the right. Every bar will have its high, open, low and close prices that happened during a specified interval that is normally defined by a trader. For instance, taking a trader that is opting for a two minutes interval bar chart(other measures than time still exist, like number of transactions called tick charts), then a new bar will be established after every two minutes, showing the open, high, low and close price for each and every minute of the interval specified. Bar charts are responsible for indications of both the upward and downward movement where the price moved and the manner in which it moved during the bar establishment.

Below are some of the keywords that you are required to comprehend from the bar charts.

☐ Open - This is the foremost price traded on the bar establishment and is indicated by a horizontal foot of a chart.

☐ High - The highest price possible traded during the specified interval assigned to the bar and is usually indicated by the top of the vertical bar.

- Low - Low keyword is the least price traded during the observed interval time for the bar and is usually indicated by the bottom of the produced vertical bar.

- Close - Close is usually the last price used for trading during the selected interval bar and is most commonly depicted on the chart by the horizontal foot on the right side of the bar.

- Range - the range is obtained by subtracting the top value from the bottom value of a chart's vertical bar. Range of bar = high − low.

- Direction - The direction the price moves during the bar is indicated by the location of the opening to that of the closing foot. A situation where the closing foot is bigger compared to opening foot, then definitely the price made an upward progression during the bar and on the other hand, If the closing foot is lower than the opening foot then the price made downward progress during the bar.

- Candlestick charts.

A candlestick is made up of three divisions namely; the body, higher shadow, and the lower shadow. The body is definitive from its green or red color. Every candlestick is a representation of a segmented period of time. The candlestick's related data will basically summarize all executed trades during that interval period of a specified time. A candlestick will have four data points namely; the open, high, low and close.

Below are some of the keywords common in candlestick charts.

- ☐ The **open** is the very first trade for the specific period and the **close** is the very last trade for the period. The open and close keywords are considered the **body of the candle**. The **high** is the highest priced trade and **low** is the lowest price trade for that specific period.

☐ We have the high being represented by a straight line to a tail, wick or a shadow from the top of the body. The low of the candle is defined as the tailor lower shadow, represented by a vertical line extending down from the body. When we have our close being higher than the open then the body will eventually be colored green that symbolizes net price gain.

When our open is reflecting higher than the close, then the body eventually will be colored red as it signifies a net price decline.

Candlestick tends to present much of emotion as seen by the wide use of colors:

- Hammer candlestick.

This is a type of candlestick that normally takes place when market security drops significantly than its opening price but however struggles to close near the opening price. It is normally in the shape of a hammer where the shadow is double the size of the real body.

Some of the important things to point out:

☐ A hammer is normally a recollection against the trend.

☐ It does not show you the movement of the trend.

☐ The background of the market is more essential

than the hammer.

• Shooting star candlestick.

This kind of candlestick is sort of a bearish reversal chart which is made up of a long upper wick, little or nonexistent lower wick and a small body. In technical analysis, the shooting star pin bar is composed of a single candlestick.

The bearish shooting star is more powerful because of its higher opening price as compared to the closing price.

- Bullish engulfing candlestick.

This type of engulfing candlestick formation represents that bulls that are in full control of bears. The green body (bulls) covers completely the red-bodied candle (bears). This normally shows the readiness of the market participants to drive a particular instrument's price higher. A bullish is just a confirmation of how the participants in the market agree on at that particular season.

- Dark cloud cover candlestick.

The dark cloud candlestick referred to as a reversal pattern. Some proponents of the dark cloud cover suggest you can catch the top of an uptrend and be underway on the down move at certain points on the chart.

- Single bar pattern.

This type of bar pattern represents a single trading

day. A single bar pattern represents price activity within a given period of time. As a result, traders and investors use this chart type to spot trends and patterns.

## How to Reduce Losses when Day Trading

Day trading is made up of both losses and wins. The odds of both occurrences happening during trading are so high. We do try our best to win and in the end, we do win frequently but in the end, losses never miss too.

Below are some the ways in which we can reduce losses in our day to day training activities:

☐ Manage your risk.

Managing your risk at individual trade is so important. It is super advisable that on a single trade you should not risk above 1% of your balance in the account. Taking an account setup of $100, 000 then a trader should not stake more than $1,000 on single market trade. With this information principled out, there are zero chances that one-point loss risks the loss of everything.

☐ Consider using limit orders.

The use of limit orders is applicable for buying and selling. While the sell limit order will be used to sell stocks once it is above or equal to limit price, buy limit order will purchase it when it is below.

☐ Bottom line.

Traders should always understand when they have intentions to enter and/ or exit a trade before execution. By applying stop losses cautiously a trader usually minimizes huge losses while avoiding the number of counts a trade is usually dumbed needlessly.

☐ Setting up stop- losses and take- profit points.

A stop-loss is a point at which a trader has preset as a mechanism to stop his/her losses by disposing the trade at a loss whereas take- profit point being inverse is the actual price point at which a trader will cash in on the trade taking the profit already acquired on the margin difference.

A stop-loss occurs when a trader had experiences that had not been planned. The points are designed to curb the "give it a little time" mentality of trading while limiting the unintended losses before they rise higher. On the other hand, take- profits occurs when the additional upside is limited given some risks.

☐    Establish a daily stopping point.

As you set up some general strategies, decide on how much you are willing to risk per everyday trading session. Remember if you make the choice to set your stopping point based on average trading performance, the amount of time you are expected to lose is higher over a span of period as you continue to learn and master new styles during everyday trading sessions.

☐    Take a wide look at your expected return.

Implement the formula in several day trading occurrences and compare the output and get to select the ones with the highest profit expectation rates.

☐     Put options.

Put options give you the chance to sell an underlying stock at a specified priced during or at the blink of expiration of a given option.

☐     Planning your trades.

Plan the trade and trade the plan. So as to secure yourself as the winner in a certain war, it will cost you to prepare for that. Preparing basically means setting up some strategies, really good strategies that will clearly thrust you forward and generally excel at the end game. Outline realistic strategies and at the end plan for your trades.

# Chapter 5: The Main Tools used in Day Trading

Ever come across this saying that a day trader is only as fine as the tools they are working with? In this chapter, we shall take a look at the different tools used in day trading.

## Best Software for Day Trading.

A day trading software is a term given to any software that can help in the decision making and analysis in order to make a trade. Some of the software will provide you with accessibility to the tools and all the resources needed.

A day trading software has the following basic features:

- Any software should have the functionality of allowing the setup of trading strategy in the system.

- Possess the order-placing function which is normally automated.

- Tools for continuous assessment of the market developments so as to act on them.

How does trading software works?

Day trading software can be divided into four different categories:

  - Charting. Bright day traders will normally chart their prices using different charting software. However, some outside vendors normally offer feeds with charting packages which help in the analysis of technical indicators. Most of these data feeds are normally advanced packages.

- Data. Before any day trader begins
  trading, you should be aware of the
  prices of the stocks, its future, and
  current currencies.

- Execution of trade. After sourcing
  for the data and analyzed it on a
  chart, at some point, a day trader will
  need to enter into trade. Trade
  execution requires some sort of
  trading software. A good number of
  trading software nowadays allow you
  to develop your own trading
  strategies using APIs (Application
  Programming Interface). Some even
  specifically provide trading
  capabilities that are automated for
  day training.

Below are some of the platforms for day trading you can select.

- Zacks Trade.

Zacks Trade is a brokerage day trading platform mostly for the US and international consumers. It started its trading since 2014 and its offices are suited in Chicago. This online platform is mostly for active traders and investors. Investors on this trading platform need to make a deposit of around $2500 for them to register an account with the broker. However, if you are seeking help to make a trade, Zacks is the best choice for you since it offers brokerage trades for free. The tradable securities involved on this platform include market stocks, exchange-traded funds, and bonds. On this platform, you can make market trades more than 91 exchanges in different countries.

The cost per share of the commission is around $0.01 with a minimum of $3. This platform is mostly preferred to the active and options traders, investors seeking to trade on foreign stock exchanges and also those who want to access a human broker.

Zacks Trade offers two types of accounts; Zacks Trade Pro normally for the active users and Zacks Trader for the retail traders. Zacks Trader has a simple user interface, therefore, making it easy for the users to navigate through the system.

The pros of this software are that:

☐ It is quite rare to find a trading platform that offers cheap commission such as a cent. To engage in trading the penny stocks, you will need to pay around 1% of the trade's value with a minimum cost of $3. The cost for options is around $3 for the first contract and cost of additional ones which is 75 cents.

☐ Zacks normally offers investors with the accessibility to 26 research and 87 reports on subscriptions.

☐ This software is also available for Linux users. Account-holders can also access Zacks using their mobile phones unlike it is seen on other software.

☐ Zacks Trade is so safe and secure. Clients normally have their own platforms from the management and they register for their accounts with unique usernames and passwords.

☐ Good customer service. This platform enables day traders who use their smartphones to trade for a free 24/7 hour basis. It is mostly for traders suited in Asia, the US, and Australia.

The shortcoming for this software is that it offers slightly higher charges on shares as compared to Interactive brokers.

- Interactive Brokers.

This software is strongly advisable for advanced and frequent traders. It charges $0.01 per share with no minimum investment required. It offers a wide range of investments such as European bonds for the government and the corporate. Interactive brokers offer research for free to its traders from around 100 providers such as Zacks and many more.

The advantages of this software include:

☐ The low commission charges on exchange-traded funds and stock tend to favor the frequent traders. The low rates also favor the margin traders.

☐ Interactive Broker's workstation is fast and offers great features such as watchlists, real-time monitoring, and advanced charting.

☐ Another great advantage of Interactive Broker is that it offers its traders massive accessibility to research and news services which keeps them up to date.

The greatest shortcoming of Interactive Brokers is that traders find it hard to navigate through the website. This makes it difficult for traders to identify the costs associated with the commissions and fees.

- TD Ameritrade.

This is one of the largest trading brokerage software with the basic and Thinkorswim platforms. It charges fees of $6.95 per share and no minimum investment is required. The Thinkorswim platform allows clients to customize color schemes and layouts according to their choice of preference. Trade tickets are found on both of the platforms so a trader can enter an order in whichever platform you are using.

After the software development team made updates on the tools and content of this software, there has been an improved look on both of the platforms making it more responsive to the client's devices.

TD Ameritrade offers a range of tradable securities; over 300 exchange- traded funds are free of charge and over 12,000 mutual funds. It also provides investors and traders accessibility to research for good quality trade execution especially for traders using the Thinkorswim platform.

The pros of TD Ameritrade include the following:

☐ Offers wide news and research abilities to the traders which keep them up to date.

☐ Provide a full range of investments such as forex and bitcoin futures trading for the right clients.

☐ Provide massive education support for the

traders. There are videos and also articles that provide simple guidelines to the traders on how to use the tools provided. It is so difficult to find a trader who cannot use this software despite you being a guru or a newbie.

☐ TD Ameritrade offers mock trading accounts. Traders are given virtual money of around $100,000 for practice. Traders can back test trading strategies and access foreign futures.

The biggest shortcoming of TD Ameritrade is the high charges on commission and the exchange-traded funds as compared to other software.

- TradeStation.

TradeStation is a day training software that charges $5 per share and requires a minimum investment of $500. It normally focuses on good quality data of the market and the trade executions. Its system is well established and normally remains firm during market surges. You can establish your own system using the analysis tools and mock testing strategies provided by this software.

The advantages of this software are as follows:

☐ The platform has minimal chances of crashing down since it is a stable platform.

☐ The software feature out excellent charting tools and backtesting strategies making it the popular software.

☐ Education support for this software is at top-notch. It normally offers classes and educational videos to its traders on various topics such as margins and many others.

The shortcoming of this software is that there no cases of forex trading and international trading is limited.

- eOption

eOption is another day trading software that focuses on quality. It has a minimum investment of $500 and charges $3 per trade. The massive number of fans of eOption is mostly after the low commission and the extreme faster trade executions.

You can check out the platform before opening the account by using Paper Trading Toolset which is given for free for around 45 days.

This software has various pros:

☐ It is easy for traders to navigate through the web-based platform. The user interface is so simple and the tools provided are easier to be found by the traders.

☐ Good customer service. The platform is so stable and seldom has cases of crashing down.

☐ The cost of using this software is very low since the charge per trade is

$3. However, users for inactive accounts are
normally charged an annual fee of $50.

The cons of this software are:

☐ Limited accessibility for the traders to research
and news providers unlike in other software.

☐ Education support is not that good. The
offerings are limited making it difficult for
new traders.

- Firstrade.

This is a trading software which is free of charge
and requires a minimum investment of $0. It
began offering $0 commission to traders dealing
with options and the stock recently and for its
benefit, it offered limited tools and research for
the traders using this software. Firstrade also has
this lending program which provides lending
services to financial bodies and account holders

and they can generate income. The traders can even sell the stock with no restrictions.

Some of the pros of this software include the following:

☐ It provides a set of accounts. It has simplified English, traditional and even Chinese accounts.

☐ It has lower costs. Charges $0 for the stock and options traders.

☐ This software provides access to stocks, options and funds type of trading. The drawbacks of this software include the following:

☐ Firstrade does not provide access to forex, future and crypto type of trading.

☐ It does not have a 24/7 basis for customer support. They only operate in limited hours as compared to other brokerage trading platforms.

☐ This platform has a few functionalities
for its traders. Its traders are forced to
use functionality from other platforms

• TradingView.

This is a trading software that is free, also has
monthly charges of $9.95 for the Pro account,
$19.95 for the Pro+ account and $39.95 for the
premium account. Trading View does not
support stock options and U.S trading.

A trader can make trades on the charts and the
software will work out for you the profit and loss
reports and analysis.

Its advantages include the following:

☐ This software is of ease of use even to beginners.

☐ Offer support for a variety of
trades such as stock, forex, and
cryptocurrency.

☐ The charting for this software is easy to use and provides you with various tools.

The disadvantage of this software that turns many off is that it has no real- time news for the traders, unlike other trading software.

**Tools and Services Used for Day Trading**

For an effective job in day trading, a trader is required to possess a set of tools and services. Some of the tools required are the basic ones that you already possess such as a laptop or computer and a telephone.

Other tools that a trader may need include a charting platform and also real- time data. The tools and services needed by a day trader to be on the move include the following:

☐ Laptop or computer.

Technology nowadays keeps on changing rapidly. A trader should at least possess a good laptop or computer with excellent memory and processors. A good computer processor will speed up the trade executions for excellent trade results. Also, a machine with high memory will have the capability of backing up the market data and there will be minimal chances of the computer crashing down.

☐ Charting software.

Day trading software provided by companies or outside vendors normally have different features. Some software has charting platforms where traders can keep track of the price changes of the stock. Price charts make work easier for traders making their work effective and efficient. Software that lacks charting platforms makes it tough for new traders making contributing to slow trades. A day trader should mostly prefer software with charting platforms.

☐    Internet.

Internet is one of the crucial resources required by online users. The Internet with fast speed produces effective work. A trader is able to be up-to-date with the current prices in the market. Workflow also becomes smooth since there is no lagging behind web pages unlike it is seen on slow internet. A trader should, of course, set high priorities for service providers with good internet speeds for excellent works.

☐    Telephone.

In case you need to cut down the costs of the internet, a trader is advised to possess a cell phone or a landline. A telephone will assist you in contacting your broker in case your offline. You will need to back up the broker's contact number on your telephone for assistance.

☐    Real-time market data.

Market data constitute of prices and markets you choose to trade. The market can be futures, options, forex, and even stocks. It is upon you as a trader to decide on the type of market you want and contacts your broker. Some brokers offer all the market data for free but with high commission.


☐    Broker.

A day trading broker can be a company or small brokers. A broker provides a trader with the necessary market trades according to your choice of preference. Different brokers provide software with different features. Some may include platforms with all trades others with limited trades. Software with all trades most times requires payment of high commission ending up being a big burden for the inactive and small traders. It is mostly advisable to select smaller but regulated brokers who provide lower commissions.

**Key Parameters in Day Trading**

Despite the trading strategies, the key parameters in day trading to put into considerations are as follows:

☐ Day trading volume.

This is a great day trading metric that helps traders identify the liquidity of an asset. High day trading volume help traders enter and go out of position so faster and easier.

☐ Liquidity.

Liquidity is a crucial parameter for day traders who make profits from many trades. Traders normally monitor the trading volume of the market trade to determine its liquidity.

☐ Price volatility.

This is essential for traders to monitor the price fluctuations in the market. Traders are able to monitor profits from prices that are short term.

**Essential Tools Used for Day Trading**

The a-must tools that a serious day trader need to have included the following:

☐   Trading platform.

With the emergence of modern technology, online traders should possess online trading platforms. These platforms are normally provided by different companies and have different features. These platforms should be advanced and firm with no bugs. There is trading software available on smartphones and users can access anytime and anywhere. You should choose software that is cheaper and will not burden you.

☐   Monitors.

Having access to multiple computer monitors is an added advantage to a day trader. Computer monitors help in keeping track of the performances of the stock, price fluctuations, news and also the key parameters. This promotes the effective performance of a day trader in the market.

☐ News and data feed.

Possession of multiple computer monitors and an advanced trading platform will definitely keep the news and data feeds up to date. Out of date news feeds bring confusion and wrong information about the stock performance and prices in the market.

☐ Research skills.

A trader needs to have marvelous research skills. The skills will help you understand the capital for the stocks market and the key parameters needed for day trading.

☐    Faster Internet.

High-speed internet is so crucial for any trader making a living with day trading. Such a kind of Internet makes work easier since trade executions become faster. Day traders normally require up-to-date news and data feeds and therefore slow-speed internet is so risky for online day traders.

☐    Capital.

Like any other kind of business, capital is a required necessity. Day traders need sufficient capital for the trading volume. This will enable traders to manage their volumes accordingly for better profits.

# Chapter 6: The Best Strategies used to Make Profit

Strategies make up a viable plan that is set to be used in any potential project. Let's dive into several sections that make up most of the strategies:

## What Type of Day Trading is Profitable?

What kind of day trading assets are much profitable? Below are some of the popular markets:

☐ Forex markets.

Forex markets are normally carried out on the margin. What I am trying to say is that you can have more trades than what you have as a deposit. This could possibly contribute to high profits on the business. Additionally, it depends on your day trading strategies and how you handle the risks in the business.

☐     Stock markets.

Stock markets are so popular that you basically buy and sell shares of a company.

☐     Options markets.

A trader in options trading can make a profit either by being a buyer or a seller. An options buyer can make a profit when the stock becomes higher or lower than the fixed price. Whereas an options seller makes a profit when the asset settles above or under the fixed price.

☐ Future markets.

Future markets are also a profitable type of day trading. It depends on your experiences in trading. Also to be profitable in this type of trading depends on the strategies you have employed in trading.

## Rules to Be Successful in Day Trading.


☐ Strictly follow your trading plan.

A disciplined life is sure of a successful life. After you have outlined your intended plan, be sure to be strict in following up. Being self-disciplined in your set target makes you ambitious and chances of being successful in the future are definitely high. A miss at your discipline is a great downfall, follow your desired motives step by step and erase the idea of getting rich quickly because it is a poisonous thought.


☐ Learn every single day.

Each and every person has a different way of learning. Make sure you set proper learning methods strategies.

Below are the most widely used methods
of communication:

- Videos.

Videos are said to be popular because they are much practical. They outline the structural and visual learning about a particular topic and enhance much comprehension.

- Blogs.

Blogs have become a great source of information because they provide detailed and reliable sources of information. To identify the best blogs out, try googling and also counter check the blog's rates before you commence reading. Find the highly rated kinds of blogs and highly interactive depicted by the presence of a couple of comments.

- Learning by forums.

Well, forums are a kind of medium where opinions and different angles of views concerning a particular problem are openly discussed.

- Portable Document Format (PDF).

PDFs are easier to find one from the internet and download it right away. They are pretty much available, reliable and easy to go through and also make some modifications. There are different kinds of PDF with different kinds of information. Always double-check whatever you are reading.

Remember to pick your PDF that goes hand in hand with your level of expertise. For example Day trading for beginners PDF.

- Online courses.

Online learning has become a dominant kind of learning. Youtube channel has become a favorite online learning channel for many people. The Internet is generally flooding with basic to advanced courses for like every field in any interest in this world. Look up to such educative videos. Explore the kind with a maximum number of views and discover the possibilities that are just about to unfold.

Remember to record(takedown) any kind of viable information that happens to be so important and outline the right steps expected to be established. This is the kind of strategy needed to produce large chunks of profits in the future.

- Books.

Books are made of pages.

Pages contain a page of any information concerning the topic in question. Okay, I am trying to justify that books contain quite a lot of information because of the number of its components. This implies that books are quite detailed and can be a good option for beginners because all they first need is quite some information.

☐ Charts.

Charts are good graphical measures at day trading. They symbolize the progress and every activity taking place during day trading. They monitor and help in examining the day trading events and aid to set up several possible likely to happen.

☐ Do something irrelevant once in a while.

Well, too much of something can indeed be

poisonous. Take yourself out and do something totally different to enhance peace of mind and better future performances.

## How to Be a Successful Day Trader

Let us look at some of the strategies and rules that need to be mastered and take into action so as to hit the major end goal; making large chunks of profits. Here we go:

☐ Monitoring the trend.

Trends are a graphical measure of the actual activities that are taking place in the day trading market.

Any trader closely following up the trend makes him or her informed and accurate in his or her levels of predictions and chances are that winning may be their middle name. They are able to purchase when the prices are high and short sell when they drop. Analyzing trends has several assumptions in that, if there are continuous cases of rising prices, possibilities are that they will constantly happen and vice versa.

Remember that day trading is not about heroes and losers, it is all about patience and persistence. Honey, try to be patient and persistent.

☐ News on trading.

News always comes in two ways; good news and bad news. Well, good news on day trading always gives the traders and brokers a huge motivation to purchase prices at good rates. On the other hand, when bad news comes in, the traders are given an opportunity to short sell prices. This kind of strategy can be used as a great move in making huge amounts of profits at a particular season and induce high volatility rates.

☐ Scalping.

As discussed, scalping takes advantage of the small

kind of prices that happen drastically during the day trading sessions. This kind of mechanism involves getting engaged so quickly and so fast and then leaving right away.

☐   Contrarian investing.

This kind of strategy describes the assumption that prices will go up and most probably reverse and then drop. The contrarian buys during fall or short sell during the rise periods. The attitude in this kind of strategy defines that the whole expectation idea is to subdue to change and that things are to head in a reverse kind of direction.

☐   Financial management.

Capital is so lucrative in any kind of income-generating activity. There is always going to be several wins and losses. Not to sound so risky, most of the traders will not input 2% of their capital in any line of trade. Be careful in whatever you consider as an investment, money loss is ever an option too.

Also, there maybe be cases where brokers demand high rates of commissions, do not fall into that trap. That is going to cause you big time. Consider the rates of commissions demanded by brokers in the first place, because too many expenses in commissions can definitely incur low rates of profits basically meaning that losses will be incurred.

☐   Proper time management.

Day trading is a journey. A certain market trading journey, meaning that for it to be called a journey, a particular process is established. A certain planned time span is encouraged. Monitor everyday trading move that occurs and will occur for it makes you learn and experience all about day trading. Good things take time, mastering the day trading occurrences is quite an investment. Remember those good investments imply good rates of profits.

☐    Consistency/ Stability.

Another point to add, day trading is quite logical. Day trading can not be analyzed by fear or even greed. Mathematical approaches have to be considered. Set strategies have to be put in place too! Examine every logical operation bound to happen during day trading so as to possess certain clear stability. Once stability has been established, expect some big-time profit rates and an excellent reputation.


☐    Timing.

The trading market becomes volatile every single trading day. Experienced traders have mastered the moves and so they are quite sure about what steps to take next once they get to read the structures. For beginners? Quite not sure of what move to take. A slow but sure protocol is fundamental too. As a beginner, do not be quite in a rush to predict. Take one or more time to examine every single trend and get your desired prediction. Do not be too slow though, you may end missing so much.

☐   Momentum.

This kind of strategy defines revolving around new sources and also identifying the substantial trending moves at high stake. You basically should basically maintain your current position, be alert with the reversing signs and face a totally different direction.

☐   Strong focus on one particular market.

Many traders become overexcited and want to trade with all markets. This should not be the case, you will end up being confused not knowing which trade to focus on. It is normally healthy for the business when you decide and focus on one trade, be good at it. Focusing on many trades at a go will make you lose.

☐   Trading pivots.

Trading pivots come in when you buy low at the end of the day and you sell at the high end of the trading day. Once you get to master these tactics, chances are that you will be an expert in comprehending the volatility of the market and therefore declare yourself successful using this kind of strategy. However, trading pivots are not the kind of day trading to be implemented daily.

☐   Select a good trading software.

To be successful, always choose a stable trading platform. A platform that provides some features such as charting tools and tools for analysis. Such software will make your work easier and you will be able to stay up to date as compared to systems that crash down frequently. Do not forget to consider the cost of the software and how legit your broker is.

☐   Risk Control.

For beginners, it is highly recommended that they engage in trading infrequently as a way of avoiding too many risks. The essence of this is to help them master their moves and learn a lot. Day trading is not just about profits only, it is about taking each day as a learning trading progress. Predict the trends at least after some minutes and not just seconds. I am familiar with the adage that declares that, commit many mistakes to learn highly, but honey, this is some real cash being retrieved from your pocket, you can become poor any minute. Slow but sure steps are highly recommended. Take each trading day as a lesson. With this, tricks and knowledge are so equipped and with no time you will be so okay.

☐ Passive position management.

A novice day trader is prone to adjust their target and stops abruptly because of being controlled by certain emotions. These kinds of emotions are caused by the sudden updates of the figures and trends on the screen that keep changing with time. This is so confusing for the beginners and after all causing them to alter their predictions hence leading to a great downfall. Only highly experienced and confident day traders can analyze the updates because they may actually know what they are doing.

For the novice day traders, leave the targets and the stops on their own, and learn how you would passively control all these. Reach for some paper material and sketch and assume how the aftermath would be without interfering with your active trends. Do some in-depth examination and comprehend why every move is happening. In the end, compare what you would have affected your trading account if at all you altered the previous trends. This is a learning process. Do this for quite a while and within no time, day trading becomes your all-time income-generating hobby. Yes!

☐   Protect your capital.

Losses are normally involved in almost all businesses. Despite that, try your best and protect the capital of your business. This can be achieved by shunning from all unnecessary risks that come along in businesses. Trust me, this will definitely bring success to your business.

☐ Risk reward ratio of 3:1

Comprehending the proper 3:1 risk-reward ratio is so important. This kind of ratio reward encourages a trader to lose small and then win big despite the frequent times you lost on the trading platform. The moment you gain some wide experience, the risk-reward ratio gets higher and higher, meaning that you are slowly advancing and enjoying some good profits. This is the kind of measure we need to strategize to grow as traders.

☐ Patience and persistence.

Plan your trades and then trade your plans. This kind of strategy defines the behavior where most traders do not really trade daily. They have this kind of paradoxical behavior where they just check up on the trends without necessarily acting up because of the fear of outlining the wrong prediction.

Well, this is not really a way of learning. Day trading calls for patience and persistence where several wrongs did are part of the journey and learning happens a lot through that. Plan carefully your trades and then predict, see how this goes. Be patient and persistent in every move you make. After all, good things always take time.

□   Hard work.

Day trading requires you to be hardworking

for you to be successful. It is not like the

entertainment business which you can joke around with. It needs maximum practices into trading and discipline. You have to be trading frequently and stay updated on the stock price fluctuations.

The above-discussed strategies help to improve time factors, skills, financial management operations, to grow as a person, risk management and most importantly, you get to learn.

# Chapter 7: The Tips and Tricks used for Day Trading

Like any other job, day trading requires you to learn the tips and tricks for you to ace it. Many are the traders who fail to finish through day trading because they failed to follow on the few tips and tricks or had no idea of them. Do not worry if you are a newbie in this, I will guide you on how to do it in the right direction.

## Tips for Day Trading for Beginners

For you to be an expert in something, it is a prerequisite to be a beginner. Below are the few tips and tricks to employ in day trading for you to succeed.

☐ Have a plan with you:

A trading plan is a set of policies that guides a trader on its activities. It is a necessary tool needed by all individuals. You always need to have a plan for everything you are working on. As a beginner in day trading, you also need to have a plan on how to do your trading.

A plan entails how, when and why to do your day trading. It will guide you on what action to implement to attain a certain number of sales or even profits for your trading. A trading plan will alert you when you are on the wrong path and you will be able to correct yourself so quickly before it is too late.

□   Make use of demo accounts.

Most day trading software normally provides mock accounts for their traders. You should take full advantage of them. Before getting into the real accounts, practice trading with the demo accounts, at least they provide virtual cash.

They also provide tools such as charts which you can read on the price fluctuations. Charts improve the performance of a trader a lot. Know the tricks in trading using these accounts and perfect your skills. After that, you can confidently create a real account with a broker and ace day trading.

☐   Have a routine for day trading.

Have yourself a routine on how to do your trading. Routine is a set of scheduled activities for any individual. Review your market trades effectively and efficiently and make sure they align with your trading plan. Scheduling yourself will make you organized and you will be able to correct the mistakes that may arise.

☐   Never get tired of learning.

Trading keeps evolving with time. As a trader, you should not be left behind. Be alert with all that is evolving. Do a lot of research, learn from articles and videos and also be alert with the trends in trading. Study on the price fluctuations to be up to date. Big losses and market risks will affect you when you stop to learn. Though do not overwork yourself to research everything all at once. Go at your own speed and have the basic knowledge on day trading.

☐    Be responsible.

Responsibility and self-discipline are a must to succeed in day trading. What I mean by being responsible is by taking the correct actions on the mistakes that arise and learn from the mistakes. Never ignore the mistakes, you will terribly fail. Also, make sure that what you do is what is included in your trading plan. If it is still not working out, go back to your trading plan. Make changes to it and try again. By doing this, your day trading business will have no complications and issues.

☐    Begin with little cash.

Do not be so overexcited when starting day trading. Day trading involves lots of risks and not being careful with trading risks can make you fail terribly. When starting off day trading, begin with little cash.

Using lots of cash as a beginner can contribute to huge risks to the business. Little and reliable cash guarantees you with good profits unlike risking a lot of your money and end up losing. Always remember this trick in order to succeed in day trading.


□   Shun losses.

Losses are everywhere. They can be a nuisance sometimes in business when they occur. Some manage to be cautious enough to beat these losses but for the faint-hearted, they end up just giving up. I do not want this to happen to you as a beginner in day trading. In day trading, you need to weigh and select the securities that are safe for you. If a market trade does not bring any benefit to you, leave it and look for the one that is good for you. This will enable you to shun the losses in day trading.

☐   Utilize resources.

You need to take advantage of the resources provided to you by the brokers. The resources can be research tools, news feeds, tools for analysis, charting tools and also backtesting tools. Select software with abundant tools for easier trading. Research as much as possible to be up to date.

Read and follow up the charts to have good data on the prices fluctuating in the market. Also, utilize the news. News will keep on updating you on the market changes in terms of the prices of the securities. Analyze the different markets with the tools provided. Weigh options and definitely select the best market you can handle.

☐   Have the basics for day trading.

The basics for day trading include a good internet connection, a stable trading platform, a cheaper and a legit broker and also try your best and own a desktop or a laptop.

- Purchase for yourself a strong internet be it wired or wireless connection. This will promote fast and good quality trade executions. It will also save you a lot of time. Slow internet will slow down your trade executions and you will not be up to date on the market changes.

- A trader is advised to have at least two desktops. You can have one laptop at the start if money is an issue but the idea of having two monitors is the most advised one. If one of the desktop crashes at crucial moments while trading, you would at least have a backup and you will lose no profit. Having one monitor can be so risky and will affect your trading performance.

- Trading platforms are essential for all-day traders. Select a trading platform which is of ease of use. Choose software with a friendly user interface since you spend your time mostly in here. Also, consider the cost and stability of the platform. Unstable trading platforms can crash down anytime and you will lose all your profits and data. Choosing platforms that are expensive for you to afford is a very bad idea. Select the software with the cost that you are comfortable with to avoid spending much than the profit. Also, select a trading platform with sufficient tools. The tools will ease the trading process and will increase your performance.

- A day trading broker can be legit or fake. Know how to distinguish the two. Be aware of the legit brokers and make a connection with them. Choose a legal broker with reliable software and less commission. Some brokers can be hard on you by charging a high commission on your trades. You need to put your profits into consideration since the main aim of all businesses is to make a profit. Also, select a trading broker who is near you or within the same country so that you can get assistance whenever you are in need.

    □    Have a time schedule for your trades.

As a beginner, you need to sit down and have a schedule for the time you will be day trading. Different markets have different times of trading. It depends on the type of trading you working on. Here is a time schedule for forex, stock and future type of trading.

- For forex traders, you can trade within 24 hours. Though the best time to trade in forex markets is around 6.00 am and 5.00 pm GMT.

- For the stock traders, the best time to trade comes in two ranges of time. You can decide to wake up early and trade around 9.30 am – 1.30 pm EST or around 1500hrs-1600hrs of EST.

- For futures traders, the appropriate time for your trade is around 8.30 am-11.00 pm EST.

So be aware of the best time to make your trades to be able to grab the best opportunities. Do not just trade anytime you feel to.

☐    Have a trading strategy.

As a beginner, do not rush to learn everything all at once. Have at least one trading strategy for yourself. It is healthy this way other than struggling to learn everything ending up losing everything. That one trading strategy will help you grow, learn things with the right speed, correct your mistakes and you will definitely make it in day trading.

☐    Set your entry point.

Identifying your entry and exit points is a crucial thing to consider as a beginner in day trading. An entry point is a price spent by a trader to purchase or sell a market trade whereas an exit point is its vice versa. A trader should ensure there is a big difference between an entry and an exit point to promote growth in trading.

☐    Set realistic profits.

Do not set high-profit targets and you are just a

beginner. Set reasonable profits that are realistic to achieve with little experience in trading. Focus on how to improve your trading skills and perfect them. Trading needs patience, so relax and do it the right way. Do not rush. Beginners who rush for bigger profits end up failing in trading.


☐    Shun distractions.

Distractions are part of the game. With a working trading strategy, try your best to avoid all kinds of distractions. Distractions can come from analysts or even articles and they will mislead you on how to do things. Kindly watch out and be on the move always.


☐ Have a strong trust for yourself.

Trusting yourself is a crucial necessity for any trader. Trust the process you are facing and all will be well. Do not overread articles and watch too many videos, you will lose hope during this journey. Have the one trading strategy you normally implement at your fingertips and do what you have to do.

□  Learn from experience.

Losses are normal in businesses. Do not be a trader with a faint heart. When things do not turn out of what you expected, breathe in. Learn from the mistakes you made and improve next time. You will progress by learning from your mistakes. So do it. Do not mind what others will tell you.

□  Be calm.

Do not panic or stress a lot when the stock market begins acting crazy. Be hopeful and courageous enough to handle it in order to be successful. Fear of failure should not be part of you. Do what you have scheduled yourself to do according to your trading plan and all will be alright. Invest in other stuff in your life, do not focus too much on trading.

□  Take control of your greed.

Greed normally affects traders so much. For

instance, you can make a trade of around $30 and set your profit target at $45. You, fortunately, hit this target at first trading. You then think of setting the target a bit higher to earn more but you, unfortunately, fail terribly at the second time ending up making big losses. My point here is that you need to be patient in trading. As time goes by, profits will increase. Set profit targets according to your trading plan and avoid losses.


☐    Develop a good attitude.

Day trading is not an easy thing. Many have lost hope and gave up on it, but you should not be part of them. Develop an amazingly positive and winning attitude that you will make it no matter what. Make sure to concentrate on what is to be done and what is according to your trading plan.

If you comply with the tips mentioned above, day trading will not be tough for you.

# Chapter 8: Money Management

## What is Money Management?

Money management is not a new aspect of the financial management world. It started when there was a rise of capitalism. When the economy was under a system that was dominated by private owners, they had their private properties and gained on the profits. Money Management started in around 1600, and individuals only survive by depending on how effectively they get their income. In the present age, to be successful financially involves having the ability and the zeal to save more, and lean on investing any surplus.

Money management is a term to refer to the many ways people manage their financial resources. It ranges from budget planning in regards to their income. Money management involves planning and purchasing items that are important to you. Without planning well and lack of money management skills, the amount a person has will always not be enough for them.

Before anyone starts on the money management journey, you need to be aware of the assets and liabilities that you have. Some of the examples of Personal assets and properties are cars, home, retirement, investment, and bank accounts. On the other hand, personal liabilities are loans, debts, and mortgages. To be able to know your net worth, you should see the difference between your assets and liabilities. When the liabilities are higher than the assets, then you have a lower net worth. Having excellent money management skills, you will be able to avoid this.

Goal setting helps in Money management. Without goal setting, you will be worried about daily bill management; this can adversely affect your long term goals. With goal setting, you can have a clear view of the expenses needed to, and which needs to be cut out. A perfect example is when you have a goal of getting a car worth $30,000, your goals will be to cut down your expenses.

Similar to someone whose goals are to get a $20,000 car?

After planning and knowing your goals, start creating your budget. A budget is an estimation of income for a defined period of time — a tool which will assist you in managing your money well. With a budget, you will be able to save some cash and be able to minimize impulse buying. An example of a reasonable budget will be to allocate $250 for entertainment and miscellaneous expenses a month after settling the basic needs. If your income increases, it would be advisable to add the extra income to your savings plan and not adding it to the expenses budget.

When budgeting, you will have multiple accounts to manage. For example, you may have an emergency fund and saving accounts. By doing this, you will avoid the temptations of spending the funds on impulse buying. The retirement plan should be kept separate from the other accounts. There are different software that you can use to assist you in money management. An example of a money management software is Quicken; it helps in tracking your various accounts and ensuring your saving and spending goals are on the right track.

The different aspects of money management include analyzing, planning, and executing a financial portfolio. The financial portfolio includes investment types, taxes, savings, and banking. In business management, there are economic variables that might affect your business finances. The best Money Management skills are to be able to access and control all the factors that might affect your financial position.

You can achieve your set goals through excellent money management. A dream of owning a home without using student loans, and be able to have a stress-free life from debts. Have a better plan to be able to deal with unpredictable events that can affect your finances; like loss of employment, serious illness. With Money Management, you will be able to have some savings that will cover your unexpected events.

Internet is a global computer network that contains information and provides communication. Banking, investment, and insurance needs did not exist before. In the past days, customers had restrictions on decisions making in their financial matters, with less information on their options in their local areas. With the lack of internet connection, there was limitation and restrictions on where to find the right information. People had to go shopping for different items, like furniture and electronics. And also the purchasing of mortgages and insurance policies.

## Money Management Skills

Do you know your income expenditure?
Do you know your shopping, clothing and entertainment expenses?

Money Management is a life skill which is not in the school curriculum. Most people learn it from our parents on how to handle money.

Since most people didn't learn about financial skills

in school, you can still learn them now. Here are some of the Money management skills that you can follow to improve your skills.

## Set a Budget

Track how you spend your money. Do you spend on food, movies, entertainment, and clothes? Do you frequently have an overdraw of your bank account? If this is true, then set a budget. Check your bank statements and note down how much is your expenditure categorically. You will find out how much wastage of money you are not aware of.

## Spend wisely

Have a shopping list when you go to the grocery store? Do you first check the price of an item before putting the item in your basket? Use coupons if available. Use online resources and mobile apps to stay focused on your expenditure. Monitor your spending! By not being attentive to these small tips, you will keep on losing money. It takes time to get coupons, and It takes some effort to find coupons and writing a shopping list and checking the price of an item before buying, it will all be worth it in the long run.

## Balance your books

Most people rely on going online to look at their bank balance. By doing this, you won't be able to know how much you are spending at the moment. The best advice is to be accountable by recording all your expenses; you will have avoided over-spending.

## Set a plan

You must have a plan for you to accomplish anything. For you to go from location A to B, it won't be possible without a GPS to show the routes. You will end up driving aimlessly going nowhere.

This is similar to not having a financial plan. You will always be broke and not knowing where your money is spent on. "Where did that money go?" With a great plan, you will be able to track your money and expenditure.

## Think like an investor

The education system does not teach about handling money, mainly how to invest in growing your wealth. The rich people did not just save $500 a month; they learned how to grow their savings and invest. Turning that $500 into $1000, then into $10,000 and eventually into $100,000 and more.

By investing and growing your money, you will have secured a stable financial future. Think like an investor, and see your money grow.

<u>Have the same financial goals with your partner/spouse</u>

If you're married and you have a joint bank account, then learn to work together. You must both agree with the financial goals.

Make a budget and also see a financial adviser to learn how to invest your money. You must ensure that you have the same financial goals and stay focused.

<u>Save Money</u>

Have a strong commitment to saving your money and securing your future. You can improve your financial situation and make it better! But you need to start with the decision to do so. Make a decision to start saving your money and improving your management skills.

# Importance of Money Management

Sticking to a budget and living within your means – is proper money management. Look for great price bargains and avoiding bad deals when purchasing. When you start earning more money, understanding how to invest will become an essential way of reaching your goals like having down payment for a home. Understanding the importance of excellent money management will help you achieve your plans and future goals.

Some of the importance of Money Management are:

<u>Better Financial Security</u>

Being cautious of your expenditures and saving, you will be able to save enough for the future. Saving will give you financial security to deal with any unexpected expenses or emergencies like loss of employment, your car breaking down or even saving for a holiday. Having savings, you will not have to use a Credit card to settle crises. Saving is a crucial part of money employment as it helps you build your financial security for a secured future.

## Take Advantage of Opportunities

You may encounter opportunities to invest in a business to make more money or an exciting experience like a good deal on a holiday vacation. A friend may inform you of a great investment opportunity or get a great once-in-a- lifetime dream holiday vacation. It can be frustrating not having the money to jump right to these opportunities.

## Pay Lower Interest Rates

With excellent money management skills, you can determine your credit score. The highest score means you pay your bills on time and with low-level total debt. Having a higher credit score, you can save more of what you have and have a lower interest rate for car loans, mortgages, credit cards, and even car insurance. And there is the chance to brag to your friends about your high credit score at the parties.

<u>Reduce Stress and Conflict</u>

Paying your bills on time can have a relieving feeling. But on the other hand, being late in paying your bills cause stress and have a negative impact like shutdown in your gas and water supply. Always being broke before your next paycheck can bring conflict and, a significant amount of stress for, couple.

And, as we all know, stress brings health problems, experts say, like hypertension, insomnia, and migraines. Being aware of how you can manage your finances, so you have extra cash and savings can put your mind at ease. You will enjoy a stress-free life.


<u>Earn More Money</u>

With your income growing, your financial planning will not only include budgeting for monthly expenses but also figuring out where to invest the extra cash that has accumulated. Knowing different kinds of investments for example stocks and mutual funds, you can earn more money from the investments than what you could have made by leaving the money in your savings account in your bank. But be aware not all investments are recognized as a good investment idea, for example, offshore casinos. One of the best benefits of having investments, you can be at work earning monthly income, and your investments, on the other hand, are making more money for you.


## More saving and time

Excellent money management can assist in avoiding your finances from spiraling out of control. It is easy to be in debt if you are unaware of how all your income it's spent monthly. Effective money management means better use of your spare time. You can spend time with your family and friends, by having a clear budget, you will be able to plan for fun days out as you will have available cash to do so.

<u>Peace of mind</u>

Excellent money management gives you some level of calm and peace of mind. With your income and the savings, you can handle any financial demands with the confidence that you have the resources to handle any need that will arise.

**Best Money Managers**

When developing your investment strategy, you will find yourself seeking some assistance. A well-chosen money manager can help you achieve your financial goals. Research is vital, find the right money manager who will be the perfect fit for your financial goals. There is a lot of information you can get to be able to find a money manager. You can rely on referrals, the internet, or financial companies to get the right money manager for you. In this segment we will go through what a money manager is. How does it work? What is the difference between a money manager and a financial advisor? What is the role of a money manager? What are the pros and cons of having a money manager? And what are the fees required?

## Who is a Money Manager?

A money manager, also known as investment managers or portfolio managers. It's an individual or a firm which manages investments portfolio and provide personalized financial advice to an individual or institutional investor. Money managers offer advice to clients about the steps they should take to increase their returns.

## How does it work?

Money managers earn a fee for their services and not a commission. In some cases, a client will pay a percentage of the managed assets to their money manager. In this way, both the client and the money manager will work hard towards the success of the portfolio. Here is an example illustrating how money managers work:

Suppose Mary has $20,000 and she wants to invest the money. She will find a money manager to manage her new portfolio. Then she schedules a meeting with the money manager. The money manager inquires about Mary's investment goals, the risk if the investment is a short-term or long-term, etc.

Based on Mary's feedback, the money manager will choose a set of securities that will help Mary achieve her financial goals. The money manager will monitor Mary's portfolio on a monthly fee basis, the performance and the value of the portfolio.


What's the difference between a money manager and
  a financial advisor?

When it comes to your finances, doing it alone can be intimidating as you try to understand the game plan. You need to find the right professional to assist you in meeting your goals.

A financial advisor and a money manager have a lot in common, the two jobs are different, and they can't be handled by one person. A financial advisor is also known as wealth managers. A financial advisor understands the specifics of the client's economic life and creates a detailed investment plan, that is is also known to help the client meet their financial goals. A money manager focuses on managing the strategy your portfolio is invested in.

The role of a money manager:

A good money manager focuses on successfully managing your portfolio strategies, and should be able to meet the following expectations:

√ To consistently manage investments portfolio with their stated investment objectives

√ Appropriate risk management

√ Avoid unnecessary turnover within the management team

√ Operate transparently


What are the pros and cons of having a money manager?

When you have a financial goal, you want it to be a success. One of the ways to achieve that is by getting an expert to help you achieve your goals. Do you have some savings which you are thinking of investing? Then you need a money manager for you to achieve your goals of investing. You need a trustworthy and focused money manager. Consider a lot of things before hiring one. To be able to make the right choice, here are some of the pro and cons of having a money manager:

The pros:

Your money manager knows the financial environment

Your money manager can assist you in constructing an income statement and help you understand the market competition. With a great money manager, you can get an excellent customized financial plan and gain essential insights that will help you in your journey.


Your financial manager will make sure your money financial wisely

If there ever a time that you needed to make sure that your cash made the most significant impact, it's now. With a strained economy, there is no room for errors. Your money manager will assist you to avoid the risks and make sure your money it's spent in a way that will bring the best returns. Wondering whether to expand? If you are also thinking of increasing your investment, a money manager makes the smartest and best-informed decisions and assist you with any questions that you might have.

A money manager will free up your time to do what's most important

Your money manager will take away the stress of financial oversight, and this allows you to focus on other vital parts of life.

Your money manager can help your business function well If you run a business, the money manager

can help you with your business. To find out why invoices taking too long without getting paid, why your business is losing cash, and you are not sure where the wastage is happening. The money manager can implement control measures that allow you to easily track your money movement.

The cons:

Your money manager could be expensive

The main reason for not hiring a money manager is the cost! Your concern is a valid one. Money managers are highly qualified and experienced and usually request higher charges. Who can afford an expensive money manager when you have come a long way without him or her up to this point? The solution here is to do your research to get an affordable money manager who will give you the best quality results as well.

Performance Not Guaranteed

Although your money is managed professionally by the money manager, there are still no guarantees. In a bad market day, even the best money manager may lose money.

Lack of Control

You might not have the time or the knowledge to wisely invest your money; it will not be 100% comforting to some people to hand over control of their money to a stranger.

**What is a Money Management Rule?**

Investing doesn't necessarily need you to be an expert in the field. As a matter of fact, you don't need to be rich to begin investing. However, most people fail to manage their money because they don't know where to start. Here are some of the rules of money management to guide you through your journey:

- Have a plan

How much are you planning to invest? When do you want to invest? When do you plan to exit? You can start from the end and determine how much money you need to invest. Plan for the future, towards financial freedom.

### • Time is money

The earlier you start investing, the better advantage you will have. Time is the biggest asset you have. For every time you invest include retirement savings too. There isn't anything that can make up for the effect of compound interest. If you end up losing money in the market, there is enough time for you to recover when you need it. For example, if you invest $1k for five years, you can make equal to $1.8k or $2k in 6 years, assuming the rate of return is the same. It amounts to a 10% difference if you invest one year later.

Do you sincerely think the 10% difference is worth falling off your investment? Never use the "it's too early to start investing" phrase as an excuse to keep your money under the mattress. It's much better to begin late than never.

- It's emotional

We usually make most of our money decisions emotionally like greed, nervousness, and fear. To be able to focus on your long-term investment plan, do not check your account on a daily basis. There are regular fluctuations in the market and individual stocks. If to are making long-term investments, you don't need the stress of constant checking.

A lot of investors get fear after checking the media, and they end up buying or selling their investments at the wrong time. To avoid making such a mistake, be ready, and try to stay calm.

- Financial Goals

Set short term and long term financial goals. Grow your goals and adjust them monthly. Correct your failures and enjoy the success.

- Save Money

Saving for regular expenses like home maintenance and car expenses. It's advisable to save 5-1o percent of the net income. Save 3 to 6 months of your income to an emergency fund.

- Financial Status

Set different expenses and include your debt payments too. Compare the amount of money coming in and what's going out. Know your debts and net income.

- Set a Budget

Budget and closely monitor your spending plan.

- Record Expenditure

Carefully monitor your money. You can note down and adjust appropriately.

- Know the Difference Between Needs and Wants

To quickly know the difference, a need is something that is required for survival. For example, food, shelter, clothes, and water while a want is everything else. Wants to make life a little bit enjoyable. Put more fused on Needs first. And spend on the Wants only after you have taken care of your needs.

- Use Credit Sensibly

Consider credit for planned purchases only. Take the amount that you can comfortably afford to purchase on credit. Credit payments shouldn't exceed 20% of net pay. Don't borrow from a creditor to settle debt to another creditor.

- Settle your bills on time

Keep a higher credit score. Talk to your creditors

in advance to explain your situation, if you won't be paying your bills on time.

## Tips Used for Money Management

Money management is a delicate topic. For most individuals, it can be overwhelming and intimidating. You may have retirement savings, or not having enough emergency savings. Whatever your concern is, having a good handle of your finances is the best option. Here are some money management tips to get you started.

- Manage Monthly Pay

Know your monthly income to better manage your money. Monthly budget, including rent or mortgage payments, gas bills, and other expenses like student loan payments, can be stressful to keep track of. However, making small changes can help you reduce your debts and expenses. Add extra into your monthly payments. Another advice is to increase payments over a year, or another option is to sign up for an automatic payment program. This will assist you to save time and money every month, as payments are deducted automatically from your savings account.

- Track Your Spending Habits

Play detective with your finances. You will need to check the financial status by yourself. It might be overwhelming by limiting yourself to monthly expenses. Check out credit card statements, utilities bank account statements and also electronic payment records. Create a spreadsheet or use a pen and paper and track your expenses.

You can also categories your expenses. For example, labeling purchases as Needs wants savings and debts. You can be more detailed and categories like transport, food, and clothing. It all depends on an individual, how much weeds you want to get. After you have compiled everything in one list, get the total of every category to see how you spend. You will be shocked by the amount of money you spend on a particular expenditure.

● Design a budget

When you track your spending, it will naturally lead to the next step: creating a budget. With the numbers you have from tracking your spending, you can now decide how much money you want to go into each item in your budget. You can also scale back some areas of your expenses that you discover you're overspending. You can write a budget as detailed as you like. Everybody's budget is different. Keep the budget relatively simple.

For proper budgeting, guideline uses the 50/30/20 rule — a strategy to help you divide and allocate your monthly income. The fifty percent will go towards fixed costs example, mortgage or rent, taxes, debt and car payments. The thirty percent will go towards spending, for example, vacation and eating out. And the 20% should go towards savings including emergency fund or investing. Regularly monitor your budget. It's better to start with a basic budget than not having a budget at all. Always save more than you're spending.

● Set Financial Goals

Once you have attained your emergency savings account, you should work towards establishing financial goals. The financial goals can be short term goals such as holiday and long term goals such as saving for college, a house or a retirement plan. The mistakes most people make with their budget is they're short-sighted. Have a long term focus, have a five or ten-year plan.

For example, it's easy to get money and buy that fancy car but, you can easily forget that you have a long term plan to have kids, and this can bring new expenses. Try to anticipate those long term goals and how to achieve them.

- Set an Emergency Fund

You never know what the future will be. You could be unemployed or get an emergency. Whether you like it or not, life happens. Your emergency funding will be determined by your budget. Most financial expert's advice is saving 3 to 6 months' worth of expenses. Having an emergency fund to handle unplanned problem will help you feel more secured and prepared. Take away stressful emergencies with a financial cushion. Put your emergency fund in a savings account that is liquid and accessible, but only to be used for emergencies.

## Apps Used for Money Management

Times are tough. Whether you earn a high net income or you get by, monitoring where your money is spent. There are many ways to track your spending, how you invest and more. We use our cell phones daily, and we always have our phones in our pockets all the time, using apps to help you manage your money is the best option.

Having a good understanding of your cash flow is very vital in managing your finances. How much of your income is coming in? When does the money get to your bank account? How do you spend the money? These are essential aspects of your financial success. Fortunately, there are a lot of money management apps in the market designed to help you check your bank balance, track your expenditure and, analyze your spending habits. Plus, there are apps that will assist you in making better financial decisions based on the data from your accounts.

And the best part? You can access your financial situation on the go. A lot of these money management apps can be checked online and also on your mobile device. It's very convenient as you can take care of your finances no matter where you are.

What do budget apps do? There are two main types of budget apps. One is an expense tracker — it best-fit people who deduct a lot of items from their taxes. For example, business owners who travel a lot, people who track their meals, transportation, and, all other professions who use expenses trackers.

This app will help you track how much money you spend. You also have all the info you need when tax season rears its ugly head. The other type of budget app is the one which helps you track your bank budget, expenses bills, and utilities. These help you track your money, especially for people who manage multiple accounts and pays bills online.

Here are some of the best money management apps you should consider:

- Personal Capital

Personal Capital has excellent features to track your budget and also include information about your investment accounts. And you can easily view on tablets, laptops, desktops and your mobile. It also shows graphs of your investments, that are easy to read and track down your investment performance.

- Mint

Mint is one of the popular budgeting apps. Mint offer features like access to your investment accounts and budgeting tools. The budgeting portion is the main feature, and the investing part is little like an afterthought. The best app if you want to keep a very detailed budget. Mint also has a reminder feature to when your bills are due, and you can also pay your bills from the app.

- Acorns

Acorns take virtual change out of your account. Instead of saving it, the app invests the difference. The app helps you start investing with virtually no effort. You can use Acorns on your transactions. The app has a new shopping type function, Found

Money.


• YNAB

YNAB is an acronym for You Need a Budget. YNAB cost $6.99 per month, but they waive the first month's fee. The philosophy for YNAB is " a job for every dollar." YNAB also offers a bank syncing and support feature. YNAB can also help you set your financial goals and make the most of each dollar earned.


• Honeydue

Many couples use spreadsheets to manage their household finances. Honeydue is the best app for couples as it helps couples best co-manage their money. Honeydue helps to track shared bills; the pair can see their accounts in one spot, comment on the transactions, and build bigger and better financial goals. Honeydue has the main feature; couples can decide on how much they can share information with their significant others. This feature helps them to remain focused on their goals and not get caught in the weeds, arguing over the small stuff.

- PocketGuard

PocketGuard will help you find savings in your spending. This app sync with your accounts and enables you to track and analyze your spending, which you can use that data to help you build an excellent budget. You can identify a pattern in your monthly spending, track your bills, and save some money.

- Dollarbird

Dollarbird is an app that assists people who have issues with budgeting. This is a free app; however, it has premium add-ons. Your budget is put in a calendar form, and you can view any upcoming expenses. Other features are, you can color code transactions by category and pay you bills through the recurring transaction. Dollarbird lets you see the projected balance, so you are aware of how much money you can safely spend. The limitation that comes with this app is that the app does not sync with your bank account. With this app, you can quickly enter your transactions manually, and this means you will be more involved with the approach to your money.

- Credit Karma

Credit Karma offers you access to your Credit Report. There are several uses of this app, for example, a company can use the app to determine whether to employ you or to estimate your credit score so as a business can be able to figure out the rates that they will charge you. This app can also be used to determine your loan applications and credit cards. Credit Karma is free to users however, the app earns money by offering targeted ads based on your credit score.

## Chapter 9: Rules for Successful Day Trading

A higher percentage of individuals fail in day trading because of ignoring crucial rules. If you have made up your mind to do day trading, there are specific rules that you ought to follow to make huge profits.

☐    Have a trading plan.

A trading plan is a set of guidelines that need to be followed by most traders to guide them in their activities. A trading plan helps you in proper money management to avoid losses. Before executing a trading plan, you need to backtest and ensure it has positive results. Most of the trading brokers provide backtesting tools in their software. A working and an affirmative trading plan will guide you on how to do your things the right way for you to succeed.

☐   Set an entry and exit price.

To survive in this game, you ought to have knowledge of the entry plus that of exit prices. Day trading, like any other business, has worst-case scenarios. The entry price will help you understand when to get in while the exit point will help you to know when to get out. With the prices, you will able to plan yourself on how to handle things in terms of market disasters with no worries.

☐   Do not rush to trade when the market opens.

Have a schedule for your trading. Do not rush to trade immediately when the market opens. These are risky moments since the trades might be of the previous nights, and the market is not stable at that moment. You should know the best time to make your trade. Different market securities have a different time to trade. Do not be overexcited and do things anyhow. Have a timing plan for your trades.

☐    Have limit orders.

You are highly recommended to use limit orders in trading. What is a limit order? It is a trading order which gives you the capability to make sales and purchases in market trade at a specific price. Limit orders, unlike market orders, enable you to be in control of the maximum price you will pay for and also the minimum amount you will sell. A market order allows traders to purchase or sell orders at the current prices in the market.

A market order usually is concerned with the execution of the order made rather than the price. It will execute the order so fast with the current market price, unlike a limit order. A limit order checks on the amount and makes sure it is within the parameters of the limit order. If it does not fit within the settings, no trade executions will take place.

☐    Shun from losses.

Losses usually are part of the game in all businesses but try your best to avoid them. Small losses are sometimes not a big deal, but watch out the losses not to be continuous. You might fail terribly. Be disciplined enough and follow your trading plan strictly. Learn the mistakes you make that lead to failures and correct them.

If the losses are still there, yet you followed your trading plan, change your strategies as quickly as possible or get out of trading. To be successful in trading, you need to cut off losses which will lower your profits.

□   Accept losses.

Losing in trading is part of learning. Do not panic when losses occur in trading; accept them. Learn from the failures and find a solution. Do not despair or anything. Even pro traders experienced losses once or twice and worked things out.

☐    Take advantage of technology.

Day trading is all about competition. You should choose methods or techniques that are efficient for an excellent performance. You can implement some of the means by the use of modern technology tools in trading. The technology tools may include simple charting platforms and backtesting tools.

Most of the charting platforms have simple user interface features that make it easier to read prices on the market. Backtesting tools furthermore help traders to test their trading plans and strategies for better performance in trading. Technology speeds up trading transactions and enables you to stay up to date. Staying up to date keeps you alert on any changes in the market like price fluctuations.

☐    Be focused.

Being a focused and self-disciplined trader will save you from lots of trouble. If you want to be successful, get yourself together, have strategies and plans on how to do trading. Know when is the right time to make trades so as not to miss the golden time to do your trades. Having a schedule will keep you organized and managed. You have to follow this rule for success in day trading.

☐    Trade with money you can afford to lose.

The risks involved in day trading are huge. The money to be used for day trading should not be capital or your savings which are essential aspects in all businesses. You should instead trade along with cash specifically for trading, which will not be a big deal when you lose it and you can recover it so fast. Do not ever think of trading with your child school fees, you will be all messed up.

☐    Manage your risks.

You need to have ways on how to handle your trading risks. Do not ignore them or else you want to be a failure in trading. Be familiar with the dangers or your day trading will be out of control.

Make trades according to the trading plan and strategies, and you will ace it.

☐ Have a mindset of steady growth.

You should possess a mindset of steady growth in day trading. Most of the traders have the mentality of getting higher profits all at once after starting day trading. Rushing for huge benefits when you are not even stable will give you lots of stress. Relax, everything will work out well with time. Do the right thing at the right speed, and everything will eventually work out.

☐ Avoid using margins.

Margins enable you to leverage your funds and even extra cash that you borrow from brokers. It can also increase your borrowing power. Operating on margins is sometimes risky in trading. Margins can increase or decrease in the market. The significant risk involved in margins is its big loss that occurs when the margin falls. It makes it worse when you lose the funds that you have borrowed.

☐　　Have big goals.

You need to have stringent goals for yourself. Goals will assist you in working towards something that you need to accomplish. Visualize your goals so good and perform day trading towards them. Work hard and you will succeed in day trading.

☐　　Bear the business kind of mindset.

Businesses are involved with pretty much of things. They include profits, losses, expenses, risks, stress and so much more. Normally, it is highly recommended that that in-depth research about your business has to be undertaken and good strategies have to be laid so as to improve the potential of the business. Well, this is much similar to day trading, lay out a good plan with set strategies and learn more about your day to day trading occurrences in a bid to excel and acquire large chunks of profits.

☐    A student of the markets.

Trading markets are quite dynamic. As a trader, you ought to discover what actually used to happen, what is happening and master all the facts involved in day trading as much as possible. This makes you really informed, educated and improves your rates of managing risks. With all these outcomes, undertaking day trading becomes quite easier and chances of incurring day to day losses become limited.

☐    Developing and implementing the trading methodology. A day trading methodology is a system of methods that are laid down so as the trader can implement them in their day to day trading activities. This discourages hesitation that is mostly experienced by most traders that just try out their luck during trading without any plan and really expect the best out of it. Day trading is not a "get rich overnight" kind of engagement but a certain activity that calls for intelligence and several tactical skills.

☐    Frequently using stop losses.

A stop loss is basically a predetermined amount of risk that a day trader is willing to accept with each trade. It is normally in the form of a particular percentage or a certain trading amount, that limits the trader from exposure during trading. Most importantly, using stop losses ensure that risks and losses are limited.

☐    Knowing when to stop trading.

There exist two reasons why you should most probably stop trading; the presence of an ineffective trading plan and an ineffective day trader. Major amounts of losses are expected in an ineffective trading plan probably due to the fact that markets may have changed, market volatility may have much lessened or perhaps the trading plan is just not working out as expected. This does not necessarily imply that trading has to be terminated, but the fact that a new trading plan had to be laid and strong trading strategies set.

On the other hand, an ineffective day trader is an unwanted day trader. So as to excel in day trading, there has to be a rule; be disciplined, follow your big plan, work hard and learn, be patient and so much on. If this does not entirely define you, then chances are that day trading is not really your kind of engagement.

☐   Keep trading in perspective.

It is advisable to focus on the bigger picture during trading. Setting realistic goals is one of the ways of keeping trading in perspective. For instance, if a trader happens to have a smaller trading account, he or she should not expect some huge returns. Always work with what you have on your plate and really try to remain sensible. It is a step-to-step income-generating engagement that requires much patience and a variety of day trading skills. Also, winning and losing in day trading is really going to be such common events. When winning, enjoy and celebrate your good efforts but do not lose too much control and during the sad moments, remember that losing trade is not afar off. Stay put and focused.

☐ Trading is not entertainment.

The word has been clearly misunderstood by most traders, especially beginners. The novice should realize that day trading is an income-generating engagement and also a capital diminishing kind of activity. Remember that failing to plan is also planning to fail. Plan your strategies, learn and get your day trading journey shining all the way with just a little loss occurrence.

☐ Learn to trade options.

With trading options, a trader has to wait for a single day before money settles after a trade. The day trading options rules are T + 1. Read several blogs describing these and most preferably, check the kind that is not really advanced to avoid making it hard to implement several kinds of strategies at the early day trading stages.

☐    Know the lingo.

Several terminologies need to be comprehended before you commence day trading. Some of them include:

Leverage: Increasing the money amount behind a given trade so as to maximize the possible returns created.

Margin trading: This involves borrowing money from a broker and using the amount of money to speculate the financial markets.

Entry point: The actual price you purchase stock prices during trading.

Exit point: The price in which you sell, commonly referred to as exiting the position.

Market order: This is an order for a trade that is executed at the prevailing price.

Limit order: This is an order for a stock trade that is only executed at the bid or ask price included in the order.

Bid-ask system: This is the basic system for buying and selling of securities. In that, anyone interested enters a bid, the price they want to pay whereas anyone willing to sell enters the asking price.

- Technical analysis.

This equips the trader with the right skills needed to make the next moves in the day-to-day trading activities. By observing several charts and patterns, the trader should be informed, learning and ready to master all moves that occur during day trading.

# Chapter 10: Common Mistakes to Avoid in Day Trading

## Mistakes Done by Day Traders

Most emerging stock traders rush in the markets expecting to make a fantastic profit. Later they find out that consistently making money us to as easy as expected. For some, they get discouraged by this realization, and many people end up giving up on this. The hope if making money always attracts people in the trading world, but reality hits them when they lose the money.

There is a low barrier in the foreign exchange market; it's the mostaccessible day trading markets. It's easy to start; you need a computer, an internet connection, and a few hundred dollars. However, this is not a 100% guarantee that you will make a profit. If all the risks and costs of day trading do not scare you, then you need to familiarize yourself with some common mistakes to avoid them for successful day trading. Before you take the plunge, please consider some common mistakes you should avoid as it's the reasons as to why new traders fail:

- Less training and preparation-

Be prepared when entering the market world. Not all traders try to get the training and the preparation before they get into the market. If you swim with sharks, you should first learn from sharks. There are books available with information about trading stocks. It is advisable to study as many of these books as possible. It takes time, commitment, and dedication to be successful. This is trading and not gambling.

- Being emotional in your decision-

Most new traders consistently get losses because of having perceptions of money. Have a long term focus on trading. It's advisable checking your account monthly or yearly instead of on daily results. Luckily, you can reduce your emotional connection to money. Try small share size trading like 50 shares a trade. This way, you can be less nervous. This can also help minimize losses, less emotional distress caused by losing a large percentage of capital.


- Poor Recordkeeping-

There are many reasons as to why traders are emotional when trading stocks. A trader may feel lack they are losing control over what's happening. To be able to control your emotions, it's recommended you keep a trading diary.

Enter all your trades, print a chart, and note down the reasons for trading. Is it technical, fundamental, or a tip? The benefits of doing this are to help you make money and also to become a better trader. You might make money on your first trial, but that doesn't mean you won't make money on your next trade. You will get better after each trade. You may lose money but learn from your mistakes.

Managing money and record-keeping is essential than technical analysis.

- Lack of proper trading tools-

Trading is like an art. It requires proper tools and resources to do better work. You must have the proper tools to succeed in the stock market. Some of the tools might include educational resource, brokers, and trading software. Be equipped with these tools before you begin trading. Research and make sure that you are equipped with all the proper tools to be able to trade effectively.

- Going too big-

There are similarities between a new trader and a gambler because both a casino and a stock market has a similar appeal — the opportunity to turn a small amount of money into a large sum of money. Preparation is the first step to succeed in the markets, and proper money management is the next step. Trading strategy has the same importance as money management, and it helps you protect your capital. It also softens the blow when you lose any trade. For example, if you trade using 10% of your capital. Even if you lose, this will not affect your account from that single trade. But if you trade too big, you stand a chance of adversely affecting your account with unnecessary risks. Don't go all in even if you have a 90% win rate because you might lose everything. Manage your money correctly and never gamble.

- Learn but never follow-

You will look for a mentor to be able to learn in this trading world. Learn about the success and failure of an experienced trader. Be self-sufficient. Learn from other people but never follow them.

- Anticipating Profits-

Most new traders do not acknowledge that trade could go wrong. They start trading with the guaranteed expectation that they will make a massive profit without learning, and knowing everything about trading. Profit anticipation can be dangerous because you might end up losing all your money. It's common for emerging traders to calculate spending on their newfound profit from the trade. Study the market and how much profit you will make. The best approach is having a neutral attitude.

- Not Specializing-

A lot of people start trading thinking it is an easy way to make money. Here are different types of securities for trading; this includes stocks, commodities, options, futures, and currencies. For emerging traders, it seems overwhelming to learn all the information about the security type. It's advisable to specialize. A new trader initially fails to specialize in a segment of a market, and they risk over-engaging in all emerging hot market segment. Specialize and stay dedicated and committed to a particular category to be successful in trading. Have an edge to be successful in trading.

- Wrong timing-

A common for emerging traders to make mistakes. Even with a good idea, if a trader purchases the stock at an inconvenient price. It's essential for a trader to learn that it might be wise to lock in a profit. Smart people trade earlier, and beginners trade later.

- Naively Following Mechanical

   Systems

Most traders use technology trading platforms that offer charting, support, and back testing. This tool helps with strategies — computers assists in getting essential information about the technical and fundamental features of a stock. However, a lot of new traders make the mistake of depending on these tools before learning how they work. Thinking the computer can replace everything. And rely on the trading systems to do the trading for them. Learn about the trading signals and don't rely on the software to think for you. If you naively follow these mechanical systems to buy and sell, you will not learn anything.

- Ignorance of How to Short-

Not knowing how to use short trading strategies effectively can cause less profitable trades. Most people think shorting as too many risks. By being ignorant of how shorting works, can limit you from potential trading avenues of earning profits mostly in a declining market. It's an essential rule of trading. Many people fail to learn about shorting in their lifetime due to fear, ignorance, or unlimited risk. However, you need to know when shorting. The stock market is a 2-way street, and by now knowing how to short you will be missing part of the game. Shorting is suitable for short-term trading. For emerging traders interested in learning how to short, it's advisable to find a stock with lower prospects and not more than 50 shares. You can learn strategies of shorting without having an excessive risk by minimizing the size of a trade.

- Placing Improper Stops-

A lot of traders improperly place stop orders causing positions to be stopped early and losing more profit. The amount of money the trader loses depends on their risk tolerance. There is much incorrect advice on placing stops. The correct ways of doing this are, to place stops according to the market like the support and resistance levels and not on profit goals. The market is not rea; y concerned on how much money you want to make. The market moves within a normal range. Analyze the stock behavior, or its standard deviation before placing a stop. By doing so, you will learn where the best stop placements are. You can get stopped out about 20% time by letting the stock show you where to place the stop. The definition of a Standard deviation is the higher and lower range of an average stock on a specific period. Each stock as a single standard deviation, they are all different as fingerprints. You can use

Bollinger Bands to standard deviation, which also gives you losses and pricing projection. Using Bollinger Bands, stock pricing will be within the upper and lower ranges.

- Not Calculating Stock Risk-Reward

  Ratio-

Before establishing a position, try and calculate the risk-reward ratio of stocks. This is a relationship between an investor's desire to preserve money versus the desire to increase returns. Through experience, a trader will be able to determine the stock risk-reward profile. Here are it's three components; Stock Price, Profit Objectives, and Stop Price. To be able to calculate the Profit Objective and the Stop Exit Price, it involves several factors like Standard Deviation or Technical Indicators. For example, look for trades that give you at least 2.5 times gains than losses. It's different for each trader because of personal preferences and the trade used. Before risking a certain amount of money on a stock, be sure you can estimate the gains to be more than the risk before you make a trade. If not, move to the next stock.

- Crowded Trades-

Most times, trades can be crowded, and this means that the traders have different information, and the stock is in a different way. Traders think the stock is going to sell off, but the stock keeps on increasing higher. It's essential to know your time frame and other people's time frame for the trade. Never be influenced by others and if a stock keeps acting opposite of your expectation, then watch the size you trade and stay cautious. Always be prepared for surprises.

- Not Cutting Losses-

Not cutting losses will hold you back and

likely ruin your account. No one likes to make

a loss, but this is an important part of the game. It's a cost of doing business and holding onto a lose will only bring you more unwanted risks. Know the amount of money you are comfortable risking a then go it's a with it. Set the maximum amount that you are willing to lose and if you pass beyond that range, you will have broken your trading rules.

Learn how to be smart on cutting losses earlier and you will have a stronger chance of succeeding.

- Vengeance Trading-

The worse thing is to try to make up for a bad trade by adding more trades. By doing this, you are being emotional and that's a recipe for a disaster.

Never trade to make up a lose. Only trade when you have a solid trading plan. This will help you refrain from making a poor trade that might hurt you financially in the long run.

- Averaging Down-

Averaging down is one of the mistakes emerging traders do. The small loss can ruin your account. It's a similar thing to most traders, a trader commits to trade, and they insist on following it through. This way of thinking is terrible and can cause you a lot of money trouble. You will be digging yourself into a deeper hole if you average down because you will be losing your position.

Losing can be a devastating thing, but, it is better to have a small loss than putting yourself in a situation where you might be kicked out of a trading game. There are always many trading chances, save up your capital. Then have an excellent trading plan and another good opportunity.

You will hear a lot about people who are victories on trading stocks, but you will hardly hear about their losses. This easily lures new traders to think that they will make fast and more profit when they start trading. To be a more successful trader, you need to study and get an edge that will help you make wise decisions. Understanding that making mistakes is part of the learning process and knowing how to reduce them, will enable you to be disciplined in your approach to trading.

# Chapter 11: Day Trading Glossary

In order to succeed in day trading, you need to ensure that you understand the terminologies that are used. From the basic ones to the complex ones; this includes the ones that beginners can understand to the advance ones.

**Day Trading**: This is the act of buying stocks or shares and planning to sell them within the day.

**Professional Day Trader:** This is an individual who does day trading for a living, as their source of income. They are licensed to do the trading, and they pay costly in order to trade. That is why when opening an account you will need to indicate if you are a professional trader. As for day traders, they do not need to be licensed, since you are using your money to trade.

**Swing Trading:** This type of trading involves holding the trades overnight. They are required to hold their trades for a minimum a day. They are investments on a short term basis.

**Bull or Bullish**: This refers to the strong market when the stock is moving up. It is also used to know the position a trader is trading on. When the market is considered bullish, it means the stock goes up.

**Bear or Bearish:** This is known as the weak market. Most traders think that the stock market is expected to go down. When they are considered bearish, they end up selling their positions.

**Initial Public Offering:** This is when a company offers its IPO. Then they offer a fixed number of the share to the open market, the reason to make money. For example, a company, have 1 million shares, and when the shares cost $10 each; then the IPO is expected to rise to $100. The money is then invested in the company's growth.

**Float:** These are the outstanding shares that are available to trade with. They normally come up after the IPO and shares are released.

**Share Buy Back:** This is when a company can buy shares back after they were sold at an IPO. This will end up reducing the shares available to trade and the shareholders will then increase their value. This will also reduce the float.

**Secondary Offering:** This is the offering that is given after IPO and it will help in increasing revenue and sell more shares. The share value will be decreased and the share supply increased. This is normally not preferred by most traders.

**Day Trade:** This happens when a trader opens and closes a trade the same day and the same stock. They are supposed to follow special rules when trading.

**Beta:** It is used for fluctuation measurement and it is used as a numeric value.

It measures the stock fluctuation against the changes and movement in the stock.

**Freeriding:** This is a situation where an investor will buy security and then dispose of them before knowing the original price.

**Crossed Market:** This is a situation that is considered temporary; where the asset-bidding price is considered more than the asking price.

**Dividend**: This is the money that shareholders are paid after holding the company's share. This is termed as sharing company success.

**Divergence:** A trading concept that is formed when the price of the stock separates with the oscillator momentum and it is considered as a reversal.

**Earnings per Share:** This is part of the company's profit that is set to an individual's share and is what is used for analysis.

**Market Cap**: This measurement is used to identify the size of the company. The sizes are set as small, medium and large, and it's based on the market value to the total shares.

**Merger:** This is the union when two companies come together and become one company. There are different reasons for mergers to take place.

**Penny Stock:** This is any stock that is below the $5 mark and they are considered as a security.

**Profit and Loss Ratio:** This is the ability of measurement that a trading system has. It helps in profit generation instead of loss and it is on a percentage basis.

**Return on Investment:** This is the system that is used to measure loss or profit that comes from an investment.

**Shares Outstanding:** These are the company stock that is with the current shareholders; they are categorized as institutional and restricted shares.

**Market Trend**: It is referred to as the direction that the market is taking for a set time. This trend can be from several days to months or years.

**Volatility:** This is how the security ability is measured and it is normally calculated over a set period as standard deviation.

**Support Level**: The level when the security demand is strong and will prevent any price decline.

**Resistance Level**: This is the level whereby selling security is considered strong and will help in eliminating price increase.

**Stock**: This is the asset that will give an individual ownership in a company. You will be able to claim the assets and any other earnings.

**Price Target:** This is what is projected as the recommended financial instrument price. It is always given by an analyst and will be used to know of any stocks that are under or overvalued.

**Recession:** It is the time when the economy of a country is experiencing a decline. This is caused by different factors over a certain period.

**Mutual Fund:** This is when individuals pool all their funds and invest in securities. Securities like bonds or stocks.

**Cryptocurrency:** This is digital security that uses the cryptography concept for security purposes.

An individual can send to other people anywhere in the world.

**Equity:** It is referred to as the ownership of the asset after liabilities and all the debts are settled. This is also considered as the share ownership in all the public companies.

**EFT**: This is the acronym for exchange-traded fund. A security that is marketable for tracking bonds and any commodities.

**Ex-Dividend:** This is the date that that is important when owning a stock.

This is because it is the date you need to hold stock in order to receive dividends.

**Blue Chip**: They are the companies that are worth a lot in billions, they also pay out dividends and are known to have reliable and stable business operations.

**Bond**: They are debt in terms of investments, they are funded to corporate and government as loan for a period and charged interest.

**Capital Gains**: When a stock or option is sold at a price higher than the original cost price.

**Bull Market**: This is a situation when the market is serving on an upward trend.

**Capital Loss:** This is when a day trader sells their assets at a price that is lower than the asset's cost price. This is the direct opposite of capital gain.

**Cash flow**: This is the money that comes in and

out of the company's account. It can be for the whole business or for a single project.

**Stock Market:** This is the trade whereby individuals are able to buy or sell their stock and companies can issue stocks. Stock is what represents the company in terms of shares and equity. The main purpose of any day trader is to make money.

**Annual report**: This is a report that is prepared by the company to give the financial position of a company. It normally includes the company's information

**Arbitrage**: This is when there is selling and buying of shares to different markets and at different price points. A good example is when the stock market is at $20 on market A and $25 on market B. A day trader could decide and buy several shares at $20

from market A and sell them at $25 at market B and pocket the gain.

**Averaging Down**: This is when an investor decides to buy more stock when the price is going down. This means there will be a price decrease on the cost price.

**Beta**: This is what is used to measure the relationship between the stock price and the market movement. For instance, when a stock has a beta of 2, this means that for every two points that the market moves and the stock will move 2 points.

**Blue Chip Stocks**: These are large stocks belonging to large companies; they are known to give good dividend payouts and are of sound financial position.

**Broker**: This is an individual who sells and buys an investment on behalf of another person at a fee paid as a commission.

**Bid**: This is the amount of money that a trader needs to pay for every share for any given stock. There is a balance against the asking price and is what a seller will want for every share.

**Close**: This is the time when the stock exchange operating hours closes. That means no trading will happen at that time, the official closing hours is normally 4 pm. There could be an extension called after hours that could go up until 8 pm.

**High**: This is a milestone in the market whereby a trade will reach the maximum point in terms of price as opposed to what it was previously. When there is a record of highs, it means that a stock may have not reached the current point in terms of price.

**Index**: This is known as a reference marker that is used by traders as a benchmark. For instance, when there is a 10% return, it may seem better. But a 12% market index may not be considered good. And the conclusion would have been, it is better to invest in the index fund rather than in trading.

**Leverage**: It happens when you borrow shares with the intention of increasing the profits. You collaborate with your broker when you sell at a price higher than the cost price, you make a profit and keep it.

**Low:** It is the lowest point in the stock price.

**Margin**: It is an account that traders use to get funds from brokers in order to buy an investment. The difference between the loan and the security price is what is referred to as margin. It is considered a dangerous way of trading because when you are not sure of the outcome it can lead to losses. It is a requirement to have a minimum balance on the margin account.

**Moving average**: The average of the stock and price per share known for a certain period. The common time frames known for moving average is 50 and 200-day.

**Open**: It is the time when traders start trading; it is normally from 8 am. The pre-market hours are from 4:30 am

**Order**: When an investor places a bid to buy or sell a stock is what is called an order. It is a requirement to put in an order to be able to buy or sell the stock.

**Portfolio**: This is a collection of investments that an investor owes that is what makes up a portfolio. There is no limitation to the number of stocks a trader can have in a portfolio.

**Quote**: A quote is the stock current trading price. It can sometimes be delayed unless you use the trading platform used by a broker.

**Share market:** This is the market where there is buying and selling of shares.

**Spread**: This is what is considered the difference between the stock asking price and the bid. Also referred to as the amount an individual is willing to buy or sell t. For instance, when a trader is willing to sell at $20 and the buyer is ready to pay $18, the spread is $2.

**Volume**: These are the shares that are traded at any given time and measured as average trading per day. Also known as the shares that are purchased for any given stock.

**Yield**: It is the return on investment from a dividend payout. Computed as the divided amount paid per annum divided by the stock price.

# Conclusion

Thanks for making it through to the end of this book. We hope the book was educative, interactive,

and informative; it should be able to help you in day trading. As a beginner, do not worry about the process and the steps to follow. This book will help in understanding all that and your success is guaranteed. At this point, you know what day trading entails, the skills needs, the mistakes to avoid, what to buy and when to dispose of. By now,

you know of the strategies and approaches that are the best to follow to be successful in this trade and the trading that is profitable and how to be successful. The tips and tricks that were given will come handy and will guarantee that you make the best decisions. We hope that the main tools that are used in day trading are well illustrated. This is because they will really help when trading as they are coupled with the tips and tricks.

Practice money management when you start earning from trading and use the apps highlighted to day trading easy.